Shut Out
the
Noise
and
Connect Already

Shut Out *the* Noise *and* Connect Already

REDISCOVER MEANINGFUL CONNECTIONS IN A DISTRACTED WORLD

KRISTI TEMPLETON

KaleidOWLscope

SHUT OUT THE NOISE AND CONNECT ALREADY:
Rediscover Meaningful Connections in a Distracted World

The information in this book is based on the author's knowledge, experience, and opinions. The ideas and methods described in this book are not intended to be a definitive set of instructions. You may discover other methods and materials to accomplish the same end result. Your results may differ.

Copyright © 2025 Kristi Templeton
PUBLISHED BY: KaleidOWLscope

All Rights Reserved. No part of this publication may be recorded, stored in a retrieval system, or transmitted in any form or by any means, electronic, mechanical, photocopying, recording, or otherwise, without prior written permission from the publisher.

To request permissions, please contact the publisher at:
KaleidOWLscope
authorkristitempleton@gmail.com

Paperback ISBN: 979-8-218-61077-7

First Paperback Edition: May 2025

Edited by: Editing by Lyric
Cover by: Make Your Mark Publishing Solutions
Layout by: Make Your Mark Publishing Solutions

Contents

Acknowledgements vii
Preface xi
Introduction xvii

1	Distraction 1
2	The Importance of Feeling Connected 35
3	Connecting with Yourself as the First Step 43
4	Connecting with Others Face-To-Face 67
5	Comparison Trap - Fear and Doubt versus Love and Trust 77
6	Emotion: The Good, The Bad, And The Ugly 87
7	Vulnerability 103
8	Romantic Relationships 111
9	Life Purpose 121

Note from the Author 125
Discussion Questions 127

Acknowledgements

A special heartfelt thanks to my Self-Publishing Assistant, Monique Mensah, for providing the inspiration and wisdom to guide me through the process of transforming this book into something tangible. Your mentorship has been a driving force behind this work that kept me focused on my vision.

I would like to extend my heartfelt gratitude to my editor, Lyric Dodson, for their supportive guidance and expertise throughout the journey of bringing this book to life. Your insightful feedback, meticulous attention to detail, and encouragement have made all the difference. I am deeply grateful for your dedication and commitment to helping me share this message with the world.

To my three wonderful children, Andrew, Abby, and Ethan. You have taught me that strength shines brighter than any challenge, and you continue to motivate me to evolve into my best self. You continuously fill my days with joy, laughter, and endless love. May this book remind you of the light you bring to each other's lives and the resilience that blooms in the face of adversity. You are an inspiration, and your journey is a testament to the power of love and hope.

Preface

I was in the middle of writing this book when the 2020 coronavirus epidemic hit. It was a time when we were all forced to abruptly stop connecting face to face with others at work, school, public places, in homes, and even outside at playgrounds. A time when human interaction dramatically transformed. In good ways and in bad ways, the pandemic forced us to find unique ways to spend our time alone and with our families, the most prominent being via Facetime and Zoom.

Almost all of our social interactions became dependent on technology and screen interactions overnight. These isolating circumstances invited us to lean into self-discovery, but many fought this opportunity, leading them to feel powerless, out of control, and disconnected and fostering a desire to rebel. Without deep introspection, this sole method of digital connection could not be sustained long-term and, in my experience, led a lot of us toward a sense of disconnection that still stings on a deep level. As humans, these feelings of disconnection can often cause hopelessness, severe anxiety, and depression.

The pandemic demanded that we learn healthy coping mechanisms and discover our internal power for our own survival. We had to find a way to live our mundane yet unknown lives with a sense of faith and hope that would allow us to persevere and develop profound resilience. It was a time when a spiritual grounding anchor was our solace, encouraging us to have faith and lay low until the difficult time passed. For those without a spiritual belief to lean on, comfort could be found in recognizing the powerlessness of the situation. Many people, including myself, went through phases of finding humor, lightheartedness, and joy followed by emotional breakdowns that brought on individual growth, a transformation through the storm of change and uncertainty that aided us in discovering the true importance of living in the present. Day by day, we waited for our normalcy to return.

Through this challenging time, connection became a priority—whether it was a stranger along the trail that my kids and I walked daily or someone we sparked a conversation with while waiting in the ridiculously long lines for restocked items. Simple conversations turned into deep, meaningful connections. Discussions about how their "normal day" would have looked were followed by how we all felt now that our lives had been swept right under our feet. Conversations about how their families were handling this time, and how difficult it was for extended family members because we couldn't physically be present in each other's lives. The challenges that come with blended families sharing two different homes, and how they could only control the circumstances under their own roof. Even in the most volatile past relationships, this sudden feeling of powerlessness created such a strong desire to do anything we could to create the best outcome for everyone.

This sudden change in our social interactions drastically transformed our dynamic, and prompted many to vow never to take the simple day-to-day interactions with a stranger for granted. These simple pleasures would forever be seen as the most valuable gift we could receive.

This was also a time when I was going through a divorce, a personal hell for me while I was trapped with my soon-to-be ex-husband and our innocent children. His late work nights and frequent business trips previously created an absence that had become my norm, so having him home all day every day was suffocating. I felt like every move I made might create manipulated evidence to use against me in our divorce proceedings. The pandemic proved to be my trial run, a time for me to solely rely on myself to be the best care-taker, chef, teacher, and nurturer for my kids as I could. It was an opportunity for me to discover personal strength that I had never truly given myself credit for, and I prayed that this very challenging chapter in my kids' lives would not burden them with more anxiety than necessary.

I prayed that their parents' inability to communicate and seek common ground would not influence them into thinking that this was how marriage should be. And if anything, I believed that my kids would transform the experience into a time of learning and discover that we can either choose how to pour into our relationships or recognize that certain connections in life only cause more toxicity, disagreements, and depletion. I hoped they would recognize when it's time to separate from those people when we no longer feel connected and nurture the connections that make us feel good. I truly believe that witnessing their parents' failed marriage allowed my children to become experts at what NOT to do in their relationships.

Above all else, 2020 taught me that the power of human connection is more vital now than ever. This pertinent desire to be seen, heard, and supported is a human necessity. And for me, I learned one of the most important things about myself: my true identity as an extrovert who valued real connections in life. From this personal experience, I believe the 2020 quarantine was one of the most challenging times for my fellow extroverts who thrived by communing with others. It was almost debilitating for me. And the circumstances in my marriage, along with this reality, exacerbated this.

I have spent the years since, which I refer to as my "post-divorce stage," living through many ebbs and flows of my own personal connections. Ironically, the times I decided to sit down and add to this book were moments when I felt most disconnected from others, when the dark holes of doubt and uncertainty consumed me, when I was feeling misunderstood, restless, unheard, and unseen. These were moments that forced me to rediscover who I am, what

I want in my future, and the importance of self-care. This is what finally convinced me to take a leap of faith and publish this book.

I hope this book provides you with some much-needed insight on how we all can do better when it comes to connecting with those around us. Even through times of loneliness and disconnection, we can lean into profound personal growth that encourages us to seamlessly and authentically connect with others.

Introduction

Most of us can probably remember the first person we genuinely had a connection with beyond our family members or family friends. The first real friendships that we independently developed as children: the pure unadulterated connections. Try to think back on what sparked this particular friendship. Perhaps it was a common interest such as a sport or a particular toy or hobby you both favored. It could have been a personality trait or their ability to make you laugh. Maybe it was how they treated you and how they made you feel when you were with them. When spending time with them, you could be your true self. They were someone who made you happy just by their presence.

These kinds of connections seemed easy to make as a child, but as adults, it can be a challenge to meet people who make you feel completely comfortable in your own skin. In our society, there's so much pressure to act a certain way or say the right thing due to our conditioning. We're taught to worry how others may perceive us, which causes us to feel a need to impress and appease others. We say one thing when we really mean another. We water down our personality so we don't seem like "too much" to others. We convince ourselves to not follow our passions because family and friends expect something else from us. But when we succumb to this mindset and don't feel completely comfortable in our own skin and confident enough to speak our truth, we tend to feel discomfort.

In this current social media era, anyone can look perfect behind a screen with filters and editing and retouches. It all becomes a façade of who we want to be, and unfortunately, this creates a fracture in our ability to form true connections with humans in person. When our perception and understanding of someone comes from their social media presence alone, we don't get the opportunity to truly get to know them. Their profile effectively creates a first impression of them before we even meet them in person! Of course, many social media influencers have begun to expose their honest truths, hardships, and faults rather than putting out a fake persona, but there's an aspect of social media that seems to drive many away from true human connection.

What does your social media stage set for others who follow you? Do you only share highlighted reels that lead people to believe your life is perfect, which, in turn, creates a false sense of intimidation and inadequacy in them? This massive shift in the way humans connect—in person versus behind a computer—has been so fast that our brains have had to rewire a categorization system within our personal connections. Within the last decade, our brains went from coming in contact with maybe twenty to fifty people a day to being able to feel somehow "connected" to thousands on a daily basis when scrolling through social media. Even walking along the busy streets of New York City, you would probably walk by hundreds of people simply on your way to work, but you would know nothing about them unless an effort was made to have a conversation.

Connection is defined as a relationship in which a person, thing, or idea is linked or associated with something else. Distraction is defined as anything that prevents someone from giving full attention to something else OR an extreme agitation of the mind or emotions. The irony between these two definitions is that, in this era of the digital world, we can easily be provided with both of these things. The easy "connections," i.e., hundreds of "people you may know" simply a click away on social media platforms, can be used as an easy distraction from our reality. This act of scrolling through others' lives and adventures while we merely fantasize of what our life could be can quickly become very toxic and draining. And there are so many people falling into this comparison trap and the dangerous feelings of inadequacy.

Whether we use connection and distraction to our advantage or allow them to control our lives is completely up to us. So how do we decipher between quick and TEMPORARY distraction, potential motivation to improve our own lives, and the tendency to develop an unhealthy addiction that leads to scrolling and posting our lives away?

With this new era of digital social connections, our brains are so overwhelmed with a need to decipher names of people, how we met, what they do for a living, their families, etc. that it's no wonder we can't seem to have a pure authentic connection with a few people on a deeper level. If we are relying solely on "keeping up" with our truest friends via social media or even texting each other, what impression can we make on future generations and the importance of deep connections?

There have been instances in my life where I run into someone I know and my brain immediately thinks of what I'm going to say, ask them about, and how I will be portrayed within the conversation. And most times, these particular instances are either when I am not feeling my best or when the person on the other end of the conversation appears to lead a perfect life. I find it's best to approach these in-person interactions with a sense of no pressure—being unapologetically myself while allowing them to do the same. When we have something in common, whether it's through our children or even something they saw me post on social media, I am able to respond in confidence knowing who I am when I remove a false fear of judgment or need to justify who I am. If you have a bigger than life personality and leading conversations brings you joy, then own it! If you are shy and quiet and being around people feels intimidating to you, don't allow a false pressure to socialize block you from being present.

We have an ability to create peace and safety within connection every day. Sometimes simply listening without responding is still connecting and possibly even serves an unseen purpose in nurturing someone's peace. You might learn something new from this conversation in what they say, or you'll find it's better to simply allow them to speak without judgment or negative reactions. When you feel confident in what you believe while giving the other person space to be themselves fully, you have the power to determine whether a connection is true to who we are and helps us grow or whether it's one-sided and sucks the energy right out of us (we will talk more about deciphering between these types of connections in chapter 4). But we also have to remember the person on the other side of the conversation may have experienced things differently.

We seem to have become "re-wired" in our ability to connect and form immediate impressions of the people we meet. New research actually suggests that all it takes is a tenth of a second for someone to form a first impression! This just goes to show that we truly do live in an instant gratification era of constant distraction with less true connections with the people around us. And while I believe making a first impression is certainly important, a second glance can reveal much more about a person than meets the eye. Usually the second, third, or even fourth impression we have on someone has more to do with our own introspective work and an ability to recognize the purpose for this connection in our life. Before we can actually see someone for who they truly are, sometimes we must see the reflection of our own bias and insecurities.

In summary, the way we connect nowadays is entirely different from how we once formed bonds. We can't always form a true connection with others based on a single first impression or what we see behind a screen, and we certainly can't build a meaningful relationship when we aren't able to identify with our own self-image and our personal opinions of others. If strong, deep connections are what we want, we must remove the negative bias and self-sabotage patterns. We must remain humble in our pursuit of learning something new every day while growing in that knowledge, and we must avoid "keyboard wars" when someone on social media has a differing opinion than you. Cyberbullying, negativity, and misinformation are spreading like wildfire, and I am convinced it's because people lack self-realization, confidence, and interpersonal skills. The beauty in life is that we aren't meant to act and think the same way, and sometimes a different perspective from differing experiences brings a very necessary light to the conversation.

Although doom-scrolling or responding to trolls on social media appear to be harmless entertainment, we have to recognize how conversations and content from others affects our thoughts and emotions. When you engage with others online, do you feel connected to your true self? Are you learning something new that could positively impact your actions and words? Or are you creating more negativity by falling into the comparison trap or scrolling through videos that only ignite fear and powerlessness in your true potential?

This new way of connecting with people could become a terrifying problem for the next generation. What will communication look like? What will relationships be like? Will mankind be able to sustain the ability to procreate and nurture a traditional family unit if we can't even form genuine connections with each other?

The intent of this book is to guide you on how to use emotional intelligence and interpersonal relationships to your advantage in this digital landscape so you can transform every experience in life into an opportunity for self-discovery and show up as your true self regardless of the noise around you.

Distraction

I am a believer in truly reflecting on every chapter in our lives in order to realize that they all in fact serve a purpose in our growth. The difficult and even the stagnant "boring," experiences could all have profound meaning if we allow them to. We have to recognize how each part serves a purpose. Rather than attempting to control every outcome and experience, we have the ability to analyze and apply the lessons we learn from each chapter and experience. By mastering the ability to accept every emotion that is generated through our life's lessons, we are better able to see purpose that comes from the good and even the bad events in our lives. Certain distractions in life can be seen as opportunities to grow. Let's take a minute to explore the avenues that lead us down the path of distractions and how they can in fact provide purpose.

Distractions as a Parent or Role Model

There were times as a mother when I found myself constantly distracted. The never-ending chores, messy house, unfinished crafts and school projects. The continuous knocking at our door with several other kids waiting on the other side added even more distractions that shifted my mind into an unbalanced sense of time management in my responsibilities. The constant "kid drama," as I like to call it, led me to fall into a perpetual trap of doing what I was good at: nurturing and teaching all these children, including my own. The meal preparation and cleanup, homework, extracurricular activities, carpooling to all their activities, etc. consumed my life.

But when I took the time to encourage the children to be involved in whatever mundane task I was trying to complete, while remembering to breathe in these fleeting moments with my little people, I realized that these moments were what mattered in that stage of life. It was necessary to truly connect and relate to these little people while enjoying the daily lessons wrapped in the mundane day to day routine. They are, in fact, the most important humans in my life. So while it may have appeared to be "a distraction," it was my own internal shift of seeing the opportunities to create "little helpers" and empower them to feel part of the daily tasks that allowed me to spend my time more wisely and create boundaries for times of day when friends could or could not come over.

I remember a day when my son took it upon himself to write and hang a sign on our front door that read, "Please do not ring the doorbell or knock on the door" without being prompted by me. Even at the age of seven, he was learning how to create boundaries in his day when he needed time for himself without distraction.

This put things in perspective, and then I realized parenting young children is really not a distraction in life. Even though it can be difficult to find balance in parenting, it is my entire life, and these precious memories and lessons we learn together are what mold and prepare my children for adulthood. This time with my small children would not last forever. I hope my kids and I will look back on this time and know that our connections with each other were always trusted and true and that we accepted each other for our differences, even when emotions were high. That, as their mother, I would forever have their back, even when they become responsible, independent adults. I wanted to make sure that memories of their childhood would remind them how to truly love and pour into the people in our lives while building an understanding of differences. That both connecting with others and creating boundaries are necessary in being true to yourself.

During my time as a stay-at-home mom, my relationship with my children and my desire to be involved in their development and experiences defined me. It wasn't until later in my life that I recognized that something was indeed being neglected: my own sense of self. After going through a divorce in 2020, the perpetual shift between full "mom mode" and an empty nest when my children stayed with their father was extremely difficult for me. It made me realize that my time with my kids had defined who I am. I had to come up with a plan to redefine myself even when they were not with me. The time spent away from them felt empty and frozen at times, which forced me to work on myself internally so I could be the best version of myself when they came back. I had to walk through and transform an overwhelming sense of guilt that led to extreme self-doubt, anxiety, and an immense fear of judgment for being a single mom.

Without experiencing one extreme of emotion, I would not have learned how to truly be thankful for the opportunities to dive deep into the patterns that had been holding me back in life. I had spent so much time concerned about what everyone else thought of me that I had never truly loved or recognized myself. I allowed myself to become so distracted in people-pleasing and always serving others that my own true happiness was solely based on others. I had allowed myself to be "mother" rather than myself, and honestly, that wasn't fair to my children. I know there have been times when I come across someone I know and can only remember the name of their kids and have to refer to them as "so and so's mom." We can't define our happiness or our worth based solely on who we are connected to or the words and actions from others in our lives. That is a lot of pressure to put on another person.

You have likely heard the adage "If momma ain't happy, no one is happy," but I have noticed that many mothers fear appearing selfish and taking time for herself. Even if you aren't a mother, nourishing individual happiness is necessary to feel safe and secure. It is important that we all attend to ourselves and our personal happiness. Here are some questions to ponder when considering how to find your own personal happiness:

1. Recognize the patterns in life that no longer serve you or that you have outgrown (e.g., negative self-talk, seeking external validation, doom-scrolling on social media, unhealthy habits, etc.)
2. Shift your mindset with affirmations:
    a. Rather than I hope, say "I WILL. . ."
    b. Rather than I need, say "I HAVE. . ."
    c. Rather than I can't, say "I am determined, and I CAN. . ."
3. Find value in each day and form a plan to make sure your time is spent nourishing yourself. Have the courage to ask for help and know that doing so is actually helping those that you love and teaching them to find a balance between responsibility, caring for others, and caring for self.

While a divided household was not the ideal situation, it provided me with moments to eliminate distractions and stop and reflect on how I needed to improve and connect with myself. I knew that my kids would only be little for a blink of time, so the time spent discovering myself was necessary for my life's purpose. Still, tons of questions flooded my mind. *Would they resent the time away from me? Would they suffer during the time without their mom fully and physically present?* I soon realized that these questions were a result of fear and insecurity. The time my children spent away from me was actually necessary for my growth as an individual.

Even in traditional families, mothers need to build time in their day for self-discovery and healing. The most challenging part of this is deciding how this time should be spent. What is it that you've longed to learn, accomplish, or create? As we engage in these nourishing activities, our children will watch and notice how to harness their own gifts with passion. This makes a profound influence in their own ability to take on the world.

Even though the "kid drama" and constant need for play seemed tedious to me, it's actually their own experience of learning how to connect with others. The daily details in life are just as important as the big picture. Especially as a parent.

I could write an entire book on how important this "distraction" of mothering small children can be for their own personal social development.

It's such an important job. Even though I felt like my career was halted due to motherhood, I realized that my children are only small and innocent for a short amount of time. We should be modeling healthy connections, most importantly connection with self, and giving our children opportunities to practice on their own.

Even if you aren't a parent, being a role model to your nieces, nephews, cousins, or even your friend's children provides an exciting opportunity to teach them something new that could spark a new passion within their own hearts! Learn to use distraction to your advantage. Find the joy in the chaos.

On to another piece of the distraction puzzle: our everyday decision making. Another continuous component of mothering children!

Distraction of Day-to-Day Decision-Making

I have always wondered why we spend so much time and energy making small mundane decisions (e.g., what restaurant to eat at, what to wear on a daily basis, our dentist, doctor, etc.) rather than executing that decision. While it's important to spend time weighing the pros and cons of each decision, we have to be able to accept the fear of possibly making the "wrong" one. We are social creatures who crave the opinions of others. We want to know the best reviews for restaurants, doctor offices, lawyers, etc. We are more likely to choose something based on our friends' experience.

Statistical data might prove one choice to be logically "the best"; however, we typically are more swayed to make a decision based on personal stories and experience, the more vivid the better.

This goes to show the importance of connections with others. Even the opinions and experiences of people from a Google or Yelp review, whom we do not personally know, can prove to be an efficient method to make a satisfying decision. This natural desire to connect with others' experiences can make some decisions relatively simple if we can keep four things in mind:

- Will this decision matter in five years?
- Will I have an opportunity to change this decision in the future if I am dissatisfied?
- Am I making a decision based only on others' opinion, or does it match my desires in life?
- Will this decision affect others besides myself?

Day-to-day decision making can be mundane. The big decisions in life (selling your home, moving far away, changing jobs or even careers, going back to school, deciding to start a family) require a bit more time and effort before making them since others are directly impacted by those decisions; however, we must also remember the why behind our personal desires. As a recovering people-pleaser, most of my decisions were made by me asking others what they wanted, accepting their decision, and then developing a sense of resentment later on for not speaking up about wanting something different. I have become much better at stopping and asking myself the questions I just shared, making sure I speak up for what I want while also being open-minded to how decisions, even when they feel "wrong," led me to more self-reflection and growth.

As long as we go through our days making choices that match our life's vision with an understanding of how change can provide growth in our lives, we will be able to simplify our day and remove the daily distraction of fear of the unknown. Before making a big decision, reflect on the following:

- Why am I making a decision (e.g., experience, improving yourself, monetary reasons, changing things up)?
- Is this decision based solely on what others want, or will it add to my life as well?
- Am I only listening to the ideas and opinions of others or am I also considering myself?

Once you've considered these questions, take a moment to recognize the feelings that came up for you when making the decision. Did you choose based on guilt, people-pleasing, or attempting to impress others? If so, face the fear of backlash and hurt feelings and speak up for what you want. You deserve to enjoy the outcome of your decisions instead of feeling forced to choose something that drains you.

On the flip side, I also find that allowing someone else to make decisions can foster a sense of trust and partnership, whether it's in a romantic relationship, friendship, or family dynamic. When we let someone else take the reins, it can strengthen our bond with them. In a world where we are constantly bombarded with choices, the decision-making process can become exhausting, leading to what is known as "decision fatigue." When we give up the responsibility for making certain decisions, it can provide a mental break and restore our sense of ease. The act of delegating some control can be a sign of comfort and mutual respect, as we trust the other person's judgment. This can result in a feeling of connection and support, reinforcing that we don't have to carry every responsibility alone.

I even find myself allowing a stranger to make the simple decisions for me! I will often just ask the server at a restaurant or the barista at a new coffee shop about their favorite menu item and order the same for myself! It not only gets me out of my comfort zone by trying something new, but it tends to brighten their day knowing they may have introduced me to my new go-to treat!

Whether it's about where to eat, what to wear, or where to go on vacation, allowing someone else to call the shots can actually offer significant relief for several reasons. For some people, decision-making is inherently stressful. The fear of making the wrong choice, feeling overwhelmed by options, or worrying about disappointing others can add unnecessary stress to an otherwise simple task. Many people feel the pressure to make perfect decisions, especially when the outcome has consequences. By allowing someone else to make the decision, we remove that stress, knowing we don't have to shoulder the burden of potential regret or second-guessing. The decision is taken off our plate, which can lead to greater relaxation. Those with perfectionistic tendencies might find freedom in letting someone else make a simple decision by removing their desire to find the perfect choice and then simply enjoy whatever outcome is chosen for them. When someone else makes a simple decision for us, it can open up a new world of experiences we may not have considered on our own.

Spending less time and energy on the distraction of constant decision-making will allow us to focus more on the important things: authentic connections with the people around us. Don't become too distracted by the simple decisions in life, but rather see them as opportunities to learn about other's experiences.

Distractions rooted in Feelings and Emotions

Overwhelming feelings can become quite a distraction as well. These feelings are inevitable in life. It's a matter of how we can recover from them and continue to thrive. Rather than playing victim and feeling like a failure, it's important to see the light at the end of the tunnel and have true understanding that mistakes happen. Oftentimes, feelings of remorse, failure, and disappointment are natural lessons in life. Don't let them knock you down to the point of not getting back up and trying again.

True connections play a vital role in pulling yourself out of ugly feelings. Many of us have experienced some degree of depression and anxiety that suddenly creeps into our lives and consumes far too much of our precious time. When we fall victim to these suffocating feelings, this can cause a rift in all aspects of our lives, leading us to abandon our authentic connections and let the feelings take over. It's a vicious cycle. Whether it is feeling rejection after a break-up, feeling failure after a project at work falls through, feelings of inadequacy after being denied a position in your career, feelings of grief and anger after losing a loved-one, being vulnerable enough to admit when you need help and support is the strongest action step we can take.

Whether you realize it or not, a simple phone call or interaction with another person can open an opportunity to not only pull yourself out of a funk, but it could also bring purpose to another person's life. We are here to offer one another guidance while experiencing the difficult times in life. We spend far too much time hiding and even numbing the ugly feelings rather than experiencing them with others. Many people on this earth can relate to what you're going through and would not turn away from helping you manage.

We become stronger through challenges, but how can we live a life of purpose if we aren't willing to be vulnerable enough to share our personal moments of hell with those we trust, therefore transforming the distraction of emotions into an opportunity to connect? Even if they don't appear to understand at the moment, this opportunity for open communication and honesty will spark a sense of compassion that builds a foundation in trust and relatability through life's struggles. These foundational elements can help strengthen relationships over time, especially through life's challenges. The key is persistence and patience—allowing space for empathy to grow and for people to internalize the message, even if it doesn't happen right away.

The most profound authors, artists, and genius inventions have been born through times of turmoil. Shifting a negative feeling through productivity can be a powerful thing. But we also have to remember when certain experiences and stages in life take time to feel, heal, and recognize that it's ok to slow down and take care of yourself without productivity involved. Avoiding your feelings by staying busy may seem productive in the short term, but this will only fester or even create avoidance in your connections and can allow even more distracting feelings of guilt, shame, or even anger to take over. My understanding between the differences with guilt and shame is solely based on whether we are taking ownership of our mistakes. While both guilt and shame are often triggered by actions or behaviors that don't align with our values or expectations, they differ in terms of how we relate to ourselves and how we move forward. When I find myself feeling guilty about something that I said, did, or may have forgotten about, I see this as an opportunity to make a change. Unlike guilt, which prompts corrective action, shame can make us feel powerless and disconnected, as if we're beyond repair.

When I have personally experienced living in shame, it was often sparked by feelings of inadequacy taking over after a job doesn't work out. I often allowed my insecurity and negative thoughts to take over. I later realized that these negative thoughts were spilling over into all aspects of my life. When I disregarded my feelings instead of taking time to reflect on the reasons for moving onto something different, I often became defensive, angry, bitter, and would push forward with more distractions to avoid accepting the internal growth. It's important to recognize that on the other side of these uncomfortable emotions is an opportunity to shift into a better version of ourselves. By giving gratitude for the experiences, lessons, and people I connected with while also taking ownership of my decision to leave, a weight lifted off my shoulders. I shifted my anger and shame into understanding that change sometimes involves grief. I learned the value of releasing anger through crying and consoling myself in moments of self-sabotage with positive self-talk like "You are going to be ok. You are strong, change is good, and you can do anything your heart desires."

There will come a time in your life when uncomfortable feelings come up, and powering through and forcing avoidance on these feelings could lead to a version of yourself that is unrecognizable. When you feel guilty about something, see it as an opportunity to change. The distinction between guilt and shame is important because guilt keeps you focused on the behavior and how to correct it, while shame often leads to a more destructive cycle of self-blame, avoidance, or even projecting blame onto others. When we feel guilty, we typically feel like our actions were wrong, but we can still see ourselves as inherently good people who are capable of change. In contrast, shame tends to erase the distinction between who we are and what we've done, making it harder to find a path forward. This reflects a healthy relationship with guilt—it motivates self-reflection, accountability, and growth. Guilt can propel you to:

- **Acknowledge the mistake**: Recognizing that something you said, did, or forgot has impacted others or violated your values.
- **Take responsibility**: Accepting ownership of the action without blaming others or external circumstances.
- **Make amends**: Apologizing, repairing the damage, or making steps to avoid repeating the same mistake.
- **Learn from it**: Guilt provides feedback, guiding you toward better choices in the future.

Give yourself permission to move on once these feelings are felt and recognized and know that the lessons through pain and even regret can be transmuted into feelings of gratitude, growth, and truly knowing what you need in life. This can be especially challenging if the pain is caused by someone in your life.

Most of the time, if someone is eager to bring you down with their opinions and disapproval, it's because they are fighting their own internal demons. It's a coping mechanism for them, and while it's not justifiable, your own growth will be diminished if you allow this treatment to consume you. I've experienced this in my life far too much. What others might see from the outside should not define who you know yourself to be. I am naturally kind, generous, and have never met a stranger. While most people appreciate my bright light, there have been many times in my life when someone tried to sabotage and dim this light due to their own discomfort. My highs and lows are extreme, so these times in my life can become very painful. I'm an open book, which means hiding my true feelings has never been easy. But being my true self has allowed many others to feel comfortable sharing their own pain and hardships with me. This is what we're here to do. There could be profound moments waiting for us if we reveal our personal pain to those we trust. Sharing our own personal experiences might allow others to heal through a sense of not being alone. We aren't in this alone, even though at times it may feel like it. Now that's powerful. Who knew misfortunes and tough feelings could become so valuable?

Recognize that when someone appears defensive, angry, or cruel, they are actually hiding pain or insecurity. We have to be careful not to become too vulnerable around someone who might have false motives against us. Typically people seek weakness in others to mask their own. This habit often allows them to temporarily lessen their feelings of shame and pain by attacking others. In these situations, when you feel you cannot trust them with your emotions, it's best to understand that their personal attacks are not about you, and instead ask them questions that allow them to share their personal thoughts and experiences: "What makes you think that?" "What have you done to solve this problem in the past?" "How does that make you feel?" Maybe by reflecting on your questions, they will be able to discover how they are handling situations in their life. In this way, you are using these moments to subtly and gently guide others through their own journey of self-discovery without remaining in their negative distracting energy.

It takes power and courage to ask these questions, especially when someone appears intimidating. And by staying true to yourself without overreacting, sometimes the ones who need the most internal healing with hidden trauma and pain will react by lashing out. In these moments, it's important to recognize how to calmly remove yourself and keep your composure.

Authentic connection doesn't happen by masking the ugly times in our lives. We shouldn't feel like our heart needs to be closed during these dark times. Our emotions shouldn't feel like life-stopping hindrances or distractions. Cracking open and living out the dark times with others is the power of influence. When you think back to the most profound public speakers and the most meaningful conversations with others, weren't they open and honest with their feelings? Most of these profound moments have probably involved tears and maybe even a tight hug afterward. Human connection and touch are more powerful than we realize. Depression can be a terrible distraction from our true potential if we try to fight it alone. We are here to guide and influence each other in profound ways. If you live with this belief every day, your power in connection can make a life-changing difference in everyone you come in contact with. We don't need a psychology degree or any sort of credibility to impact others in meaningful ways. It's actually pretty simple when you hold that power and ability to be raw and honest with those around you. You don't always have to mask your pain and weakness. When an opportunity to relate with some else's pain comes up, sharing your experience could save their life. Don't be so distracted in your fear of being vulnerable or desire to appear superior that you miss an opportunity to grow through discomfort and connect with others.

Healthy Distractions

There are actually a few healthy distractions in life. Sometimes humans need to come up with a healthy distraction or rather "coping mechanism" during times of hardships in order to ground ourselves through hard times.

The quarantine during the 2020 COVID-19 pandemic is a perfect example.

During that time, social media platforms, FaceTime, and phone calls became some of the only ways we could stay connected with one another. Taking long walks with my kids and even a quick trip to the grocery store were my only methods of staying connected to people in person. During this time, I discovered my true identity as an extrovert. I found my voice through writing, would seek comfort when outside in nature, and even taught myself to play a few songs on the keyboard. Music has always been a comfort in my life. I often listen to the same song and playlist every day as a source of control. I have since learned that this habit is actually common for people struggling with ADHD. For me, I needed some predictability and consistency during this time, which meant that our daily walks and a playlist on repeat brought solace. They were my "healthy distractions" that kept me from indulging in unhealthy distractions, like alcohol, food, or excessive shopping, to mask my pain and "feel better." I'm sure you have some healthy distractions too. I like to call them my "glimmers" and often see them as "comfort triggers." What routines create comfort and a sacred space for you? In what ways can you get out of your comfort zone and get creative with how you connect with others? Perhaps you enjoy shopping, exercising, journaling, cleaning, cooking, or spending time with your pets.

I've spent much of my life consumed by unhealthy distractions, like people pleasing, alcohol, and more, as coping mechanisms. While most of my time consuming alcohol was spent in "social settings," there was definitely a time in my life when I used it as a numbing tool. During the difficult times in my marriage, I felt so alone that drinking a glass of wine on a nightly basis turned into two glasses. I used wine to numb the doubt that crept in while attempting to be the best mom I could be in supporting my kids through their challenging lessons and experiences in building connections. Oddly enough, it was right after my divorce when I was made aware of the difference between "drinking for enjoyment" and "drinking to numb life's pain." I had hit such a rock bottom of feeling lost in the new role I had to play as a single mom that I had to face the harsh feelings I had been numbing away with wine.

We all want to feel in control of something in our lives, and predictable routines can satisfy this need. When life takes a turn that appears to flip everything upside down, discovering safe and healthy coping mechanisms can truly help us through these times. Find the power to quickly halt the unhealthy coping mechanisms before they become routine habits that can negatively impact our life's path and even the people we love. Addiction is often the fear of feeling pain. If you find yourself saying, "I need a glass of wine," or if you feel like you want to escape tasks that used to be simple or when self-sabotage and catastrophic thinking are becoming your norm, shift the thoughts into more reflective questions, like:

- What positive changes can I make to gain control while also surrendering to the pain?
- What two or three simple tasks can I accomplish in a day to grow through these hard times? (These can be spiritual connections, self-care, or just checking off a few boxes in my daily routine, whatever soothes your soul).

If a task feels especially overwhelming, make the process a little easier for yourself:

- Screenshot the email or link with the information and add it to a notes section in your phone to take care of tomorrow.
- Utilize all the to-do apps (One Note is my favorite!) and create tabs for each category of tasks.
- Set time aside to complete the more mundane tasks that you often put aside.

Now you might be wondering where and how all the "self-discovery" and healthy distractions fit into your schedule, work projects, and other responsibilities. Well, it might look different for you depending on how much time you're able to build in a day, but it can be the little times spent alone that we often take for granted:

Shopping: External things can in fact bring happiness, but ask yourself if the investment will enhance your life or if you are only shopping for others or to create more clutter in your life. If you find shopping to be a healthy distraction for you, reward yourself with a "daily allowance" for taking care of mundane tasks. By setting aside even $3 a day, you can save up for that favorite handbag, necklace, massage, or shopping spree, and you'll know you earned it!

Exercise: I personally discovered that my relationship with exercise can shift when time is limited so my false idea of "exercise" while training for marathons often led me to talk myself out of it when I no longer had time nor stamina to run. Exercise can be as simple as a walk around the neighborhood, spending fifteen minutes in quiet meditation to quiet the mind and soul, or even putting on a good song and dancing in the kitchen!

Journaling/writing: I often use voice to text on my phone notes throughout the day to jot down something I would like to elaborate on in my books or journal later. Spending time writing down my thoughts and experiences and reflecting on how it all impacts me in both negative and positive ways gives me motivation and purpose.

Cleaning/organizing/purging: I often find joy in simple tasks that create less clutter and more predictable space for me and my kids. There is joy to be had when cleaning out the clutter and even thinking about someone you know that could use items that no longer serve you. One of my favorite books about decluttering, *The Life Changing Magic of Tidying Up*, gives thoughtful insight in how we can shift our view of our things, find more purpose in what brings us joy, and let go of the things that only add more stress.

Spending time with your pets: I have met more people while owning a dog. At dog parks, walking my dog around the neighborhood, and even planned meetups where we let our dogs run free in an open field while catching up with our neighborly friends. But my cats have brought more connection with hilarious posts and laughter on social media! I don't know about you, but just scrolling through funny pet videos lights up my soul and brings healing laughter, even after a stressful day! Animals can be therapeutic family members that heal the soul just by their unbiased presence, affection, and silly shenanigans! Think about what brings you joy by owning a pet, whether it's filling a desire to nurture, teaching your kids responsibility in pet ownership, or even filling a lonely void during a new uncharted stage in your life.

Cooking: I find cooking to be a form of therapeutic art. Remove the fear of "not being a good cook," and try a new recipe! Next time you order a new dish at your favorite restaurant, Google the recipe and add it to a "recipes to try" tab on your phone so you won't forget! Half the problem for me is not knowing what to cook. Create your shopping list right away and plan a day to give it a shot! Even if it doesn't turn out as good as you'd like, every time you make that recipe, you have an opportunity to improve! Cooking can also be a form of joy, expression, and love for others in your life. I recommend the book *Bread and Wine: A love letter to life around the table with recipes* by Shauna Niequist. Not only does she provide delicious recipes, but she tells stories behind the memories created when serving these meals and how cooking and breaking bread with others is a form of connection and a healthy distraction.

Social Media and the Digital World

As I mentioned in the preface, we grew up in much smaller communities and had more predictable, long-lasting connections with people in person than generations coming up today. Community networks were consistent, and family units were far more solid. In our modern, digital world, many of us tend to be nomads, seeking career opportunities, furthering our education, or even escaping a current situation in pursuit of "the next best thing." This is where social media can be convenient in today's ever moving and changing society. We crave connection and interaction, so social media has created a method of feeling somewhat connected to the people of our past and present. Nostalgia is an important feeling that reveals memories of who you are based on where you've come from. Unfortunately for some, taking a stroll down memory lane with just a search bar and a click could potentially lead to memories from a painful past or a longing for the people we had to leave behind, but these are also opportunities to heal and feel pride in where you have come from!

I remember when I went off to college, moving away from the only place I had known as home when I was only eighteen years old was a massive shift into "practicing adulthood." Nine hours away from home, I started a new life in a completely unfamiliar community with a few familiar faces but mostly a community of complete strangers. I was no longer able to rely on the predictable interactions at a grocery store or while eating out. It was all new, unfamiliar places and people. For the introverted, this could be a solemn retreat. For me, on the other hand, I felt completely out of my comfort zone. Being vulnerable was new to me, and I often avoided making new connections that could potentially reveal the insecurities I was hiding behind the people-pleasing persona I had perfected. So, I comforted myself by eating. As a teen who created a means of control through eating disorders throughout high school, I still suffered from terrible body dysmorphia, so eating to seek comfort became a toxic cycle. This caused my self-image to deteriorate, and I lived in a constant state of lack. I entered my twenties with a haunting fear that I would never be smart enough, pretty enough, or strong enough to take on the world.

College can be a very hard time for those who haven't truly developed their sense of self. My distraction of food gave me temporary comfort, and I was consumed with planning my next comfort meal while avoiding social situations involving food that could have led to a binge and purge cycle. Eating disorders can truly take over your mind, body, and soul in this way. Overcoming this mental and physical challenge was one of the hardest things I have ever done in my life, but it led to an inner healing and acceptance in being in control of my health.

During this time, I leaned on connecting with the extreme extroverted people who appeared to be comfortable with anyone. No one was a stranger to them. This introduced me to a world of truly knowing people and a recognition that no one is perfect. It gave me opportunities to discover who I am as an empath, and I became passionate about loving people for their flaws, insecurities, and hardships, and then finding a light that had been dimmed within me for far too long. These fun-loving, carefree friends pulled me away from my fear of the unknown and gave me a sense of community, and I finally felt comfortable enough to nurture my connection with self as well as with others. I found such humor in their raw honesty and vulnerable stories without worrying what someone might think. They taught me how to put myself out there despite my imperfections and truly see the light in everyone I met. These connections saved me from my inner demons during a massive time of transition.

We have to recognize that any judgment from others is never on us! If I could speak love and hope to all the vulnerable young adults entering a new phase of life, whether it be college, career, marriage, parenting, divorce, losing their loved ones, I would tell them they aren't alone. Everyone around them is struggling with some sort of hidden insecurity and fear of being misunderstood and unseen. If we spend more time being authentic, open-minded, and loving, we can use this vulnerability as a tool to work through our own insecurities rather than falling into the comparison trap. Developing supportive relationships through life's challenging times and transitions could be the necessary shift we need in our world right now. Adulting should still be considered a developmental stage of growth. Social media was not around until later in my college experience—likely for the best. We can all agree that social media platforms, on a whole, don't encourage users to form true connections with one another. The connections that are made online are made in spite of social media algorithms, and they are a convenient way to keep in contact with friends and family past and present. It can also be a distraction we use to numb our mind and boost our own ego by fulfilling a need to affirm our own accomplishments. But despite these adverse consequences of social media, I often use it as a method to seek support during my times of struggle.

Social media has undoubtedly created a shift in the ways we connect with others. Feeling connected on social media can be important and can actually provide an easy method of staying in contact with people we are unable to meet up with in person. I know for me, after spending a long day around many different people in person, being behind a screen and enjoying a fun game, scrolling through videos, or just searching for new recipes or music can actually be satisfying. But it should not be our ONLY form of connection. We must force ourselves out in the world in small ways. Make plans to talk on the phone or even meet up with the people you've digitally connected with face to face in a public place for coffee or a meal. If used wisely, social media can boost our career and confidence. It could even be an entertaining way to share talents or spark a hobby. It's fun until it creates a sense of inferiority or even jealousy of those we follow. We must recognize when social media turns from a healthy distraction to an unhealthy one, and proactively handle it with grace rather than allowing the comparison trap to bring up toxic emotions that could rift the relationships we've already formed. We must find balance with social media and not let it control our physical relationships and reality.

Our most cherished relationships cannot be nurtured from a screen. We need human contact. It's a fact. It's how we were built. Some need physical contact more than others, but if we are isolated, we will experience negative impact. Getting out of a "comfort zone" of digital connection can be as simple as taking a walk around the mall, sitting at a busy coffee shop, or chatting with the cashiers at the grocery store. I have found that the most random interactions have led me to spark a similar conversation, whether it's what perfume I am wearing, where I got my top, or even my Texas A&M ring. We have an innate desire to feel connected in similar interests and experience. Social media can serve within these kinds of groups, like book clubs, running clubs, and fitness meet-ups, and seeing people face to face often removes a false stigma that, with practice, opens a door to feeling more comfortable in your own skin.

A growing trend that has seemed to happen overnight is furthering our education through online courses rather than in a classroom with like-minded people from all different walks in life. I find that this is creating a generation of humans who are unaware of the importance of connecting with people face to face in educational spaces. As far as I am concerned, this is creating an indirect crisis of people being unable to have constructive disagreements rather than heated arguments full of greed, selfish intentions, and negative emotions. How can we find a balanced way of educating future adults virtually while also allowing them to be in the physical field of their study? There has to be a combination of both or our future workforce will become disconnected and unable to adapt and relate with another's point of view. This harsh reality is something I feel needs to be immediately addressed.

Getting out of our comfort zones and being around people who might have different belief systems and ways of living is necessary. Not only for the importance of understanding others but for developing an empathic understanding that can lead to global transformation. We can't spend our lives living behind a keyboard. We have all seen how easy it is for some to hide behind a keyboard unknowingly destroying someone with harsh words and a false sense of power. We can't coexist happily with others without feeling like our lives are truly connected with theirs. War and hate are the result of simple disconnection and people feeling misunderstood.

As you can see, distractions in life come in many forms, but they can all be transformed into opportunities for connection. It's okay to temporarily utilize healthy distractions such as social media as a coping tool or maybe even to help others in need. But it's not okay to allow the distractions of life to spiral out of control into unhealthy habits that create an isolated world that affects you physically, mentally, and emotionally. Be sure to recognize the difference for yourself while also honoring the times when people in your life might need your connection as a healthy distraction from their life's challenges.

The Ebbs and Flows of Disconnection

We've all had periods in our lives when disconnection becomes a haunting realization. I've experienced several traumatic times in my life when disconnecting was inevitable. Trauma can come from feeling misunderstood which might cause you to think that people in your life don't agree or validate your beliefs or share a common life purpose.

There were times in my life when I felt like an outsider. When I was making decisions regarding my family's health that didn't fit the status quo of societal norms. Whether that be regarding delayed vaccination, using essential oils and more natural methods of healing, or allowing my kids' bodies the time to heal before taking medical intervention, this was not a "normal view" of raising my kids. I spent a lot of my adolescent life in "victim mode" by trying to seek attention through people feeling sorry for me. I felt victimized by the system in many ways, and what eventually happened was people saw me as weak. They also poured into my victim role, which wasn't truly adding value to my growth. When we see ourselves as a constant "victim," we aren't seeking solutions. Rather we create a life of lack rather than abundance. We don't seek solutions, therefore we don't step into our full potential on this earth. Sometimes when we fulfill a desire to seek alternative solutions and explore other options that don't seem customary to worldly beliefs, we might feel disconnected from the rest of our world and even led to believe we are a conspiracy theorist. If you haven't connected with yourself or haven't established a vision and purpose behind your decisions, you WILL second-guess yourself and constantly feel you're going against the grain on a day to day basis. This eventually transforms into playing victim in our own lives.

As I previously said, we are wired to make many decisions based on what others think and have experienced. It's human nature to want to justify our decisions, and it's convenient when we have proof from others that the decisions we are making are right. Whether we are making a drastic change in our diet to be healthier, making a big move for reasons others might not understand, or accepting a new job that has big risks or is completely out of our original field of study, these are decisions that at the end of the day, are ours to make. And for me personally, the times in my life when I felt the most disconnected were when I made those big decisions on my own and received backlash from the people in my life who didn't agree with me. These were times when internal connection was vital. We need the ability to validate ourselves by checking in with our life's main paradigm. If our decisions are made in alignment with our visions and desires for the future, then they are valid. It's important to recognize that our decisions impact others, but at the same time we can't hold back and wait for other people to validate our choices. When we make decisions that go against the status quo, there is a difference between rebellion and simply going against the grain to seek alternative solutions. Rebellion is more about active opposition to authority or a system, often with the goal of changing it. Going against the grain of normalcy is more about resisting or diverging from established norms, often without the same radical, overt opposition to a system or authority. It may simply be a matter of personal preference or non-conformity.

The key distinction is the intent and scale of resistance. Rebellion is typically more confrontational and aimed at systemic change, while going against the grain can be more individual or less direct. This was a very important distinction for me when feeling victim and fear of judgement for my unconventional ways.

The disconnection in our country over the past few years has been terrifying to witness. While it's important to stand by our individual right to make educated decisions when it comes to voting, I am not one to obsessively follow the political agendas during election time. While I do weigh their stances toward important decisions that could impact my family, I sometimes have to disconnect with the weight of my vote. Yes, this is a very controversial point of view and it's something I have realized to be more sensitive to when having conversations with others, but on the same note, I can't allow the political decisions that are made directly affect my happiness. I have not allowed my voting choices during the election to cause angst because I know politicians are not the directors in my personal life. Sure, their decisions impact the country where I live, and I won't discredit the importance of our right to vote. But I often see politics as a "them versus us" mentality, and this rift has led to poor decisions among the American people. The judgment toward those on the right side versus those on the left side causes many to feel like an outsider when their politician doesn't get elected in office. People rebel against the other side and are placed in a box of "those who don't agree with my stance," which is extreme disconnection. We have to separate political views in our relationships or else we won't have true connections.

We can no longer allow our opinions to cover our insecurities, but rather have open minded discussions with people who are open to see and respect a different perspective.

Kristi Templeton

We must live in love and respect rather than with a fear of having different ideas and opinions. It's important to remember the difference between rebellion and seeking alternative perspectives when talking about politics. Keep in mind that if your belief involves going against convention or traditional ways to the opposing argument, neither idea should aim to overturn or radically change the structure or authority of what exists. It can be an idea of non-conformity that might be more personal, philosophical, or creative in nature. Keep in mind that everyone has different experiences when it comes to feeling threatened by particular policies, political parties, and procedures put in place, and healthy disagreement whether in person or on social media do not discredit or hold power over your personal decisions and beliefs. The human heart is often the key to intuition, so if you lead with understanding, grace, and empathy versus rebellion, I believe we can all become a catalyst in uplifting humanity even in disagreement.

The Importance of Feeling Connected

As I mentioned, social media can be a fantastic tool to keep in touch with all the people we've met in every chapter in our lives. It can also be used to connect to our new surroundings once we have moved. Every time I moved to an unfamiliar place, one of the first things I would do is connect with a local group of moms or a community page on social media. I often use this outlet to find everything from a new pediatrician for my children to the best iced coffee in town. As I said earlier, we as humans crave the opinions and experiences of others, so for me, this was the best resource to navigate my new life.

While social media is a wonderful outlet for staying in touch and getting advice, the deeper, more meaningful connections in life take time and lots of effort to cultivate. Have you ever had a relationship that went from "just met" to "bestie or lover" overnight? Of course not! These relationships are an investment, and it takes time and consistently showing up. It's those little moments, the laughs/jokes, the ability to be there for someone and listen to and relate to them when they're having a tough time working through hard decisions. As humans, we need to feel connected to each other in order to be healthy and thrive. Living in isolation for too long takes a psychological, physical, and emotional toll on humans. According to the National Institute on Aging, neurologically speaking, being alone for too long can cause depression, anxiety, violent behavior, psychosis, or severe physical impairment such as high blood pressure, a weakened immune system, heart disease, cognitive decline, and even Alzheimer's.[1]

The darkest times of my life were usually when I was the loneliest. A year and a half after my divorce, I still felt so disconnected from this new version of myself. I had lost almost all the mutual friends I had prior to my divorce, and I was

---

[1] National Institute on Aging, https://www.nia.nih.gov/news/social-isolation-loneliness-older-people-pose-health-risks#:~:text=Health%20effects%20of%20social%20isolation,Alzheimer's%20disease%2C%20and%20even%20death

still attempting to make new connections with the people I was meeting during this hard time. Loneliness often puts us in troubling positions, pressuring us to relieve it by seeking out connection wherever we can, even if it's unhealthy.

The loneliness I felt after my divorce caused me to fill the void with unsustainable, lust-filled relationships that I discovered were unhealthy on both sides. When loneliness creeps in, we often feel like failures in our own life's path. It can be a dangerous emotion if we don't have self-control and the ability to decipher between true romantic connections and lust. It can lead to broken hearts and falsely leading people to believe they are capable of true love, only to toss them away like a wet blanket. It brings guilt and shame and can destroy the potential for a healthy relationship. I have seen this happen to far too many people in my life, and I can say from experience that being honest and true to another person in regard to what you are looking for in a relationship and how you honestly feel about them will usually become a positive experience for both. So how can we overcome any lustful desires we might have in times of loneliness? We can prepare for temptation and learn what our hearts can truly handle rather than acting in selfish ways that lead to guilt and self-sabotage. We must understand our worth and our power to say no, even in vulnerable situations.

Figuring out how to be alone after a breakup is so necessary and even therapeutic. How can we expect to form a deep, long-lasting romantic connection with another person when we haven't even healed the wounds created from another relationship? There may always be residual damage from a previous relationship that could creep into your new connection, but we cannot be completely dependent on someone else to heal these wounds. That's why it's important to spend an adequate amount of time healing after a breakup. This can vary depending on the length of the relationship, the level of commitment, time spent together, and how the relationship ended. However for me, these factors really weren't relevant to the pain I experienced. Feeling seen and connected to someone on a romantic level can feel incredibly fulfilling, but this isn't necessarily a healthy method for healing and moving on, unless you are willing to accept the necessary internal growth and recognize the selfish desires your potential partner might not be ready to fulfill.

So what can you do to make sure you form healthy connections while also nurturing yourself? Find what you're passionate about without anyone else involved. What do you seek in a future partner, and how can you make sure you're working toward a version of yourself who will be truly ready to let go of those connections if the time comes?

Solitude and Loneliness

I had many times in my life when I had to find comfort within my loneliness. As a result, I have learned the profound differences between isolation and healthy solitude. Solitude involves internal reflection, growth, healing, and warmth. It is finding refuge from the chaos and noise around you. Isolation, on the other hand, can become an unhealthy avoidance. Not seeking truth but rather finding fault and falling into a victim mentality of "why me," while avoiding seeking answers and internal comfort.

If you find yourself slipping into a state of disconnected isolation, discover the value in solitude. My solitude is sunshine, music, writing, meditation, good food, and relaxing without worry—healthy distractions. In these spaces, I allow my thoughts to pass without using too much time and energy overthinking. I know it might sound easier said than done, but discovering comfortable solitude requires practice. I believe there will be times in everyone's life when loneliness creeps in, but with full understanding in the full circle effect that takes place through internal transformation and removing yourself from the external factors affecting you, uncomfortable loneliness can actually be a gift that opens you up to greater self-awareness. The following is a piece I wrote in 2018, prior to divorce, when feelings of loneliness revealed the internal growth I'd need to undertake years later:

"Something happens when you're alone . . . unable to connect. Unable to relate with another person. Unable to even disagree.

You start to realize the true meaning of life is to connect. To interact, whether to agree or disagree. You learn that having strong relationships with people who would do anything and go out of their way to help is a rare treasure.

You learn when to stay in your own lane. To be selfish. Yet empathetic. Not letting haters get you down. Because you only have one life to live and it's your own.

You learn that your children—your own flesh and blood—they are who matter. And even though they may bring feelings of stress and chaos, they will be the ones by your side in the end, and your internal chaos is not their burden to bear. They are your life line, the humans who have profound purpose and are a precious gift.

Some relationships can become stale, but the gift and meaning of why a relationship is suffocating becomes clear and soon follows with what I can do: discover the pure joy, healing, and power within myself."

Dealing with Judgment

Spending your life trying to connect with every single person and making attempts at forcing them to understand you is a waste of time and energy. The true connections that matter in the grand scheme of things are what really matters and are worth your efforts in finding the time and genuine ability to pour into. The biggest dilemma in life is distinguishing the surface-level daily connections from the more meaningful people who you admire and know will serve a purpose in your journey. I was a people pleaser who always wanted approval. I think if I were told in my twenties that every person who enters my life might have an expiration date and a lesson, I don't think I would have worried and stressed so much about what everyone thought of me. We are all evolving and growing for a bigger purpose, and unfortunately there are far too many who don't quite understand this. As I was once told, "Not everyone will like you! And that's okay!" These words will forever ring true in my life, and yet it took me far too long to truly understand what this meant.

Our jobs, our children's friends, our romantic relationship acquaintances, family friends—these people serve a purpose. But it's our job to know our own true selves to recognize when to sit back and observe our interactions and when to directly converse and have profound conversations with the people we see throughout our lives. There is freedom in letting go of false expectations, being open-minded to another person's advice through their experience, and knowing that feeling a sense of judgment coming from someone else is not your burden to carry.

So next time you find yourself quick to judge someone else's actions or life path, ask yourself if this judgment is out of care and concern or from misunderstanding their personal experience and feelings. When our intentions and self-recognition are pure, we have the ability to protect ourselves when someone's actions and words negatively affect us without creating false narratives by feeding into negativity through judgment. Release the distraction of trying to appease everyone around you. They are walking out their own struggles, insecurities, and revealing new versions of themselves with a different life experience than yours.

Connecting with Yourself as the First Step

Throughout my healing experiences in life, I have discovered that loving yourself means intentionally creating a life of true happiness, love, and opportunities for success through discovering who we are in every stage and life experience. Loving yourself removes excuses and empowers us to recognize feelings of discomfort and inadequacy as signs toward growth. Becoming a better athlete, leader, friend, partner, or mother all involve some sort of discomfort and moments of wanting to give up, but if channeled properly, these challenges can lead you back to loving and accepting yourself and recognizing how far you've come. We must prioritize loving ourselves because in the grand scheme of life, we are all we have.

Sadly, too many of us live life carrying shame and fear that is deeply rooted in worry of how others may view us, which can become severely toxic. It's not a natural way of living and can take over if you don't take ownership in the power of honoring yourself. Nobody and nothing is perfect and everyone has gone through life's hardships to evolve into what might appear "perfect" to us. We must recognize and truly own our authentic selves before worrying what others think of us. It sounds so simple, perhaps even like something you already do, but ask yourself: can you truly put forth your true self with confidence in your everyday interactions, or is how you conduct yourself a facade of who you wish you were or what others want to see?

What if you had the ability to break down anyone's walls by just accepting them for who they are and giving them a sense of security in being their true selves? It can be as simple as owning up to your faults with an apology, celebrating the wins of those around you, affirming their abilities, or just asking questions to build a better understanding of how someone thinks and why they may have a negative response during an interaction. These actions are within our personal control and can help us build trust with one another on our journey to evolve into a better version of who we want to be.

I spent many years of my life not knowing who I was, worrying about what others thought and how my decisions would impact them rather than myself. I was brought up to respect my elders and avoid conflict at all cost, so I rarely felt confident enough to ask questions like why I needed to complete a task or why I couldn't embark on a new interest or hobby. I developed people pleasing, "good girl" behavior and became terrified to make my own decisions, opting instead to act based on what others told me to do to appease them.

We are given so many labels throughout our lives, but we have to know when to erase a label by acting on our own behalf and not allowing the naysayers to lead us astray while also asking the tough questions to give us a better understanding of why this label is being given to us in the first place. I was known as the "good girl" based solely on doing as I was told. I later came to discover this yearning to please was based on the positive attention I received with my "good girl" behavior.

There was an instance in third grade when I proudly spoke of how I never got in trouble and always did as I was told. A little while later, that same day, I was ordered to write my name on the board as a punishment, one I had never experienced. I looked at my teacher in disbelief. I was told that I didn't put my book away and because I was "distracted" while reading, I didn't listen to the teacher. This broke me, and I remember wanting to ask why I wasn't given a second chance. If I had heard her the first time, I would have done it right away. I cried in front of my peers and begged not to write my name on the board. Looking back, I remember the only reason I was afraid to have my name on the board was the fear of what others would think. Would they think that I had disrespected a student or even my teacher that day? I worried that my "good girl" label would be ruined forever.

Now I can assure you that this wasn't the case and that this small "penalty" that felt so grand in my little nine-year-old mind did not cause me to rebel, but I do often look back on this day and wonder if that teacher was giving me an opportunity to feel a sense of punishment by doing what I thought was more important during that time. Reading my book rather than looking up for the next lesson was not hurting anyone, but it was an act of subtle "distracted deviance" that led me to speak up for myself. From then on, I learned that it was ok to make mistakes and carry on the next day by learning how to correct what we may have done wrong the day before. Even in adulthood, we can grow through the tough emotions of shame or guilt rather than let them tear us down. The most important thing is to discern when this feeling of shame or guilt arises based solely on what others will think or when it comes up from your own act of dishonoring yourself. Speak up when you feel wrongly accused. Own your mistakes and make a change when you know you have done wrong.

When I later became a third grade teacher, I was able to create my own full circle effect by offering my students opportunities to reflect and share their personal thoughts throughout the day. The children that entered my classroom were often pre-labeled as "good" or "naughty," but would come into my classroom with a fresh slate. I wanted to know each child as an individual and would often use reflective coaching to understand why they refused to work while honoring their thoughts with choices and compromise. The new generation of children are often viewed as "rebellious" or "difficult to teach," but I can guarantee you when given the opportunity to share their thoughts behind their behavior or ideas on what is being taught, mutual respect can be built among the teachers and their students, transforming a classroom of individual students into a united group that is motivated to learn from each other. The old school mentality of "teacher knows best" no longer applies to these kids, and we as adults must create a balance in explaining why responsibilities exist and when to open the conversation to see new ways of executing goals. Children need opportunities to think and speak for themselves in order to learn mutual respect in all relationships.

With my "good girl" conditioning, I continued being uncomfortable in my own skin for many stages in life, and therefore had difficulty truly connecting with others and opening up in my relationships. This negatively reflected in all areas of my life. I was disconnected with what I wanted in life, who I was, and how to portray myself in many situations. I was a people-pleaser who probably came off as insecure and disingenuous. By continuously worrying more about what others might think and constantly seeking approval from everyone but myself, I was actually dimming my own light and the value I had in the world. When I didn't speak up for myself and just agreed with everyone around me, I was inadvertently sacrificing my needs and ability to grow through potential disagreement. This eventually led to me feeling resentment while putting more pressure on others to "call the shots" and make decisions for me.

This is why it's vitally important to start with yourself. While it's okay to be seen as a "friendly person," working toward loving and knowing yourself is the most important step in connecting with others in meaningful ways. This gives a sense of security in all relationships, removes pressure to act a certain way, and opens opportunities to learn through differences.

I have spent some recent time pondering on what causes people to make the tragic decision to take their own life. It's a confusing situation when this occurs and seems to be happening far too often with the current shift in the world we live in. I find a recurring and unfortunate trend is that these people have put a false pressure on themselves to appease those around them and fulfill a false expectation. When even a slight sense of potentially letting people down creeps in, they slip into a self-sabotaging cycle of feeling like they will never be good enough or strong enough to accomplish an expectation that truly wasn't reality. What are we doing so differently to put mankind under such tremendous pressure that they are making a drastic decision to completely end their lives?

Are you living your life with the goal of fulfilling someone else's expectation of you? If this is so, I encourage you to reconsider your motives. Your purpose is YOURS to create and navigate the ebb and flow in growing through trial and error as God intended. No one has walked a life of purpose without mis-steps and failures. The pressure to perform will always be there to transform you into a profound existence that can only be realized when you accept yourself wholly, mistakes and all, and learn how to shine a light with love and understanding of everyone you cross paths with. We are here to influence one another.

Inner Confidence

One of the ways you can start with yourself is by developing a deep inner confidence. I like to visualize a spectrum of colors when understanding the development of individual confidence. On one end of the spectrum is unhealthy arrogance, characterized by "always being right" and the inability to bend for others, and at the other end of the spectrum, there's unhealthy insecurity and general inability to voice your opinions.

Why should we spend our time acting on what others want to see? Is that true connection? While we need to consider a "filter" exposure regarding certain parts we allow some people to see and hear, the closest people whom we connect with need to see every side of our true selves. Are you shining who you are in the present while also developing the future version yourself? Do not allow fear of judgment from others to dim your light. Being your most authentic self, even if it's uncomfortable, vulnerable, or cringey at first, is what will lead us to "our people," and as I have said before, the judgment from others is not your burden to carry. Achieving a balance between shining with inner confidence and being vulnerable enough to admit weakness is a delicate but powerful act. It involves embracing both your strengths and your imperfections with honesty and grace. With self-acceptance, authenticity, and balance in your communication with others, inner confidence doesn't come from hiding your vulnerabilities—it comes from recognizing that you are worthy, whole, and capable, even with flaws and challenges. By being vulnerable, you create authentic connections and demonstrate resilience, which only strengthens your confidence.

Dealing with Your Past

The past brings us profound lessons, but it is not something we should feel obligated to bring up to those we barely know. The deep levels of transformation that brought us to our current selves are only sacred to those we have deep, meaningful, long-term connections with. We should not feel obligated to unveil any personal layers of our past to become a shadow of what we currently desire in life. Do not let your past prevent you from seeking your future. Your present and future are what matter when building new connections. With time and trust, people will come to understand how you have evolved into someone they want to know. Even the darkest secrets are understood by those who are invested and want to continue a future relationship or even friendship with you. Keeping your past to yourself doesn't mean it's something you should be ashamed of. We learn so many valuable lessons through our past mistakes and current weaknesses. Instead, see them as a gift that you can utilize to become a better version of yourself and as a marker to how far you have actually come.

Tools for Self-Discovery

Discovering who you truly are is the greatest gift you will ever achieve in life, nourishing your present self in all facets of life, including family, relationships, health, career, finances, and your spiritual belief system. Your energy will take a positive shift in the right direction and people will be naturally attracted to this. It takes courage to accept our weakest and most vulnerable side while also continuously working toward improving ourselves so we can be open enough to form authentic connections with others.

One of my favorite ways to facilitate self-discovery is a method of journaling that I was taught in a counseling session, called putting thoughts to trial. This exercise helps me get to the root of my intrusive thoughts. First, I write down how I think someone may perceive me. Then, I justify my actions and words that could be leading them to think this way, and finally, I disprove their misinterpreted way of thinking with my own truths. Over time, this has allowed me to become more comfortable with uncomfortable conversations in regard to what someone may perceive.

An example of this was a misunderstanding with a coworker of mine. I felt that her words and actions in constantly interrupting me and sharing her expertise during a therapy session for one of my clients and their family was showing incompetence in my abilities. After this session, I built up the courage to call her and explain my point of view and then ask for hers as well. This was such a vulnerable act in admitting my feelings in regard to her taking over and opened the conversation for sharing her perspective during that visit. It also gave me an opportunity to explain why her method was not the best fit in this particular case, and she was able to accept how my approach worked better for the family.

I came to discover that most of my "evidence" in her thinking was actually her helping me during that session rather than her judging me. This conversation and my own point of view was actually helpful for her to understand that there is not always a "one size fits all" approach to therapy, and how important it is to listen and reflect with families in order to see how their priorities and feelings align with the expertise we can offer. I have been through my own journey as a mother to a neurodivergent child, and I know it takes time and patience to understand and embrace the challenges that come when we recognize a child's unique needs and their different, profound ways of thinking.

This offered my coworker and I an opportunity to recognize the balance in sharing our knowledge while also making sure our experience matches what our clients and families want. Open conversations will always allow ourselves to shine a light and have mutual understanding even with different opinions and experience.

If we force ourselves to be someone we're not, we will attract those who also haven't discovered themselves. Spending too much time transforming into a different person solely based on who we are with can become exhausting. We aren't meant to be chameleons and should not be trying to put on a front every time we're around different crowds. We can all agree that it's comfortable to be around people who know us for our true selves, the good and the bad, rather than feeling the need to pretend we're always perfectly put together and have everything figured out. So why are we so afraid to be our authentic selves when true connection comes from exposing our entire being?

I acknowledge that it can be intimidating and even dangerous to be vulnerable with just anyone, which is why we have to pay attention to the types of people who bring out our best and the times when we are personally comfortable to be vulnerable. I say personally because I have put up a guard even when around the most cherished people in my life. I learned that these were times when I was battling my own internal turmoil. The times when my safety in familiarity was being threatened and my life was shifting in new unfamiliar ways. During these times, I found myself living in catastrophic thinking over the worst case scenarios and was dangerously allowing self-sabotage to take over. These times of internal discomfort often led to the "comparison trap," a mentality of "Why can't things be easier? How can I be a successful career woman while balancing time nurturing my family?" As I will discuss later, the comparison trap mentality is a dangerous place to live in for too long, but there are ways we can utilize this way of thinking to our advantage.

Unfortunately, many of us seem to be in this constant pursuit of "the next best thing" in life. It's important to remember this idea when we take others' views of us too seriously. When we put too much value on those temporary connections rather than seeking the deeper, more meaningful ones. Love and honor yourself first and the authentic, meaningful connections will come. The most valued connections come when you feel safety within yourself.

Two other helpful self-discovery tools came to me at an unlikely time. Back in 2017, I was preparing to run the Chicago Marathon for the first time. I had run Boston in 2014 and had caught the marathon bug. I wanted to run Boston again, so qualifying was a huge goal I was working toward. I just knew the second I received notification that I had gotten into the lottery for the Chicago marathon that this was my chance to qualify for Boston. Well, God had other plans. And it was going to take significant time and multiple setbacks to achieve this goal of a BQ.

While training for my first Chicago marathon, I developed a sudden injury during my final long run. It was three weeks before the race, and I literally could not run at all. The doctor suspected a stress fracture. I knew if I found out it actually was a stress fracture, this would significantly affect my mental state while trying to finish 26.2 miles. I always tell people running a marathon is 70 percent mental and 30 percent physical for me, and I have discovered that, for many other athletes, the mental doubt that might creep in prior to performing/competing is important to avoid! So I postponed the MRI until after the race. I did in fact finish the marathon, but I could not walk at all the next day. Sure enough, after the race, I discovered that I did indeed have a stress fracture on my hip.

While recovering after the marathon and having running taken from me so suddenly, I was sent down a dark road of recovery. I had always used running as my coping mechanism and "escape" when dealing with stress and anxiety, so not having the ability to run was unbearable for me. With winter following right after this injury, I sunk into a pretty deep depression. I wasn't able to escape my reality through running like I had done for so long. After my injury, the beginning of 2018 proved to be a very dark time in my life, and it caused my other connections to falter. I became physically, emotionally, and spiritually consumed with feelings of weakness, vulnerability, and had even started noticing my marriage falling apart. I blamed myself for losing a true connection and sunk into a hole. We grew apart little by little and neither one of us chose to work on growing together but rather grew apart. We forgot to build the time in for each other, and he seemed to be gone for work all the time.

And unfortunately, after twelve weeks of recovery and finally getting the green light to begin slowly running again, I broke my ankle while running a family obstacle race with my son in spring of 2018. Yep, a race meant for kids, and clumsy me jumps over a hurdle only for my foot to land smack into a small hole in the ground causing the most horrific cracking sound I've ever heard from my thirty-five-year-old body. Talk about when it rains it pours! I was once again on the mend, strictly no running, and I knew at that point, I had to find an alternate way of destressing and staying healthy both physically and mentally.

Now with the first injury, I sulked, ate my feelings, drank far more alcohol than I should have, and allowed my mental state to deteriorate. I felt vulnerable and like my strength and passion in life, running, was whisked away again with no return. Rather than allowing these emotions to swallow me whole once again, I decided to take action with my second injury. I knew this time around how absolutely important it was to NOT let my trauma and insecurity lead me down a road of negative coping mechanisms, but rather to recognize my awful feelings and create a mind space that allowed me to be a witness to them rather than let them consume me. Enter yoga and meditation.

I had been seeing a holistic Ayurvedic doctor in Massachusetts at the time. I felt so blessed that my chiropractor had referred me to her because she was exactly what I needed during my injuries: a voice of reason who taught me the importance of paying attention to my body's unique composition and dietary needs and the significance of balance. I had been a runner all my life, and my body was finally screaming at me to rest and recover. This doctor would often say to me, "This is how your body was built and always will be, which is why it's necessary to find balance and nurture what fuels your physique." She "prescribed" yoga and mindfulness while my body recovered.

While I was able to attend a few yoga classes, even a simple child's pose put extra pressure on my ankle, which felt discouraging and like I would never feel back to normal. So meditation was my outlet. My first attempt at meditation was quite humorous. I had never fully sat with my own thoughts and just allowed them to pass by. It reminded me an awful lot of the book *Eat, Pray, Love*. Her experience was almost frustrating when after multiple attempts, something that seemed so simple felt near impossible and worthless. For me, it went something like this:

Ok, I can sit here and concentrate. Kids are at school, I don't have anything to work on. Here goes. *Phone pings with a sale at Franceska's* Ooh, I need a dress for the Sole Sister banquet. I will look real quick. Oh, now I need to text Meg to plan to shop! We have to shop! *Texts friend, then sees an email from my kids' school about a fundraiser coming up* Registers for fundraiser. Sees another tab open on my phone for a yoga certification I was looking into. Remembering that I need to register for my favorite Warrior Sculpt class for the next day before it fills up. Registers, looks at my schedule to see when I work the front desk next. I need to reach out to someone to cover my shift for Andrew's school concert on Tuesday...and so begins my fight with finding time to escape the busy world right at my fingertips - on my smartphone.

So many distractions we must learn to shut out!

I feel like I discovered who I truly am by tapping into my healthy coping mechanisms during the most traumatic times in my life. Unfortunately for many, it usually takes this rude awakening to finally take the first step in self-discovery. And while it's not easy and takes practice, finding emotional solace through meditation is a divine thing. I also found a yoga class that helped me understand the true power and necessity behind meditation. It can be so valuable to silence the thoughts racing in your mind and temporarily escape the noisy world around you for even a brief five to ten minutes a day. Meditation for me, became a lifelong habit that healed my mind and soul. A key foundation to connecting with oneself. Whether through meditation, an exercise known as "brain dumping," through writing all those distracting thoughts down on paper, or stepping outside in your bare feet and soaking up the sun, get off your device, shut out the noise, and soothe your soul. Set up a "meditate" alarm on your phone and make it happen!

Another one of my favorite self-discovery tools is an exercise I do every new year. I come up with one word that will be my primary focus for the year. In 2018, "lessons" was the word I chose at the beginning of that year. Not knowing this would be the hardest year for myself, my marriage, and discovering a new path to healing, the word "lessons" appeared to be a haunting challenge, when in reality, it was actually a lesson toward self-discovery for myself. The irony in this word is when I looked back on my personal journal in 2018, the word "connection" was brought up in all my personal experiences. Looking back on this year, I also remember living in Malaysia that summer with my three babies and learning the most valuable lessons of understanding true human kindness despite differences. I looked back on my incredible surprise birthday party with my favorite people prior to 2018, spending time with my sister and best friend at an amazing concert and with my community of incredible friends in my neighborhood that had blessed me through the years leading up to this very hard year of lessons. These true connections that I had poured into actually pulled me out of that hole. They were the people who would see me through the next few years navigating a big move, going through a divorce, and the COVID epidemic. Without these connections, I don't think I would have survived the lessons of 2018.

The most influential lesson I can share is through reflecting on the reasons for your own current hard times and attempting to find some time and space for gratitude while the tough lessons are happening rather than in hind-sight. We all have lessons in life that we may have to learn the hard way, so shift your mindset into new ways of understanding growth through these lessons.

In 2019, the word I chose was Grace. There were so many shifts that happened in my life this year, including a big move back to Texas, running the Chicago Marathon for the second time, stomach issues that started to rear their ugly head, and no longer having a job as my outlet for connecting. So for me, the word Grace meant not fulfilling the "false expectations," and it became very necessary leading up to a divorce and COVID in 2020.

Self-discovery is one of the most valuable tools that we all must work on in life. If you want to create genuine connections with others, knowing who you are and what you want out of life is the first step. We must honor who we are and grow through the lessons and experiences in order to attract the people into our lives that will accept us entirely. I find that the most insecure people in life are those who are quick to criticize and judge others. Because they have yet to discover their strengths and weaknesses, they mask their uncertainty of themselves by exposing others. It's a selfish need to project their discomfort on others. Toxicity spreads toxicity, and the first step is acknowledging when you are guilty of this kind of behavior and then taking the path toward self-discovery and self-acceptance instead.

Each chapter in our lives, even the traumatic ones, molds us into who we are destined to be. As long as we accept the emotions that are generated through each life lesson and not stifle them away, we will be individually growing to become who we are meant to be. By sweeping an unwanted, uncomfortable emotion under a rug, we are denying ourselves of true growth. It's so important to choose a helpful tool that allows us to sit with our personal emotions and reflect on what has triggered us and what we can productively do to move forward and learn from each experience.

Projecting on Others

Throughout facing the deep, dark roads on our walk in life, the worst thing we can do is project our awful feelings on others. Unfortunately, there are certain personality types who feed off empaths who feel deeply for others. It's always been hard for me to understand why, but I have had a handful of instances where I felt targeted in my life. I've been told I'm a bright light that is here for a greater purpose, but I never truly believed what that meant until recently.

Now we've likely all heard the word "narcissist" at one point in our lives. Hell, I may have even had some characteristics of a "narcissist" during certain stages of my life. But I have never been someone who directly targets the vulnerable, kind, well-loved people on this earth. This was the difference I held true between myself and a true narcissist. As Brene Brown says, "Owning our story can be hard, but not nearly as difficult as spending our lives running from it."

While working at a well-known athletic club in Boston, I made a tough call not to let a guest into the club. My boss at the time took me into his office and degraded me worse than I've ever been scolded. I walked out feeling like my soul was injured. I didn't even cry because I could feel that it was his way of venting, and unfortunately, I was the one who gave him ammunition that day. Fortunately, he later brought me into his office and genuinely apologized for his behavior and understood why I made the decision to deny a guest that day. I respected my boss and was very impressed that he could apologize and admit to this fault.

It's a huge step toward healing when you can admit fault and understand that we all make mistakes when it comes to venting and projecting negative feelings on others regarding a problem that really didn't matter in the grand scheme of things. Remember this on a day to day basis before snapping at someone who is on their own healing journey. Our projections can cause greater damage than we realize. Listening is key in any misunderstanding.

Unfortunately in 2022, I was directly targeted in a toxic, narcissistic way. I still have insecurities after what I endured that have forced me to face many dark demons, even to the point of reaching rock bottom. As a result, I spent several months at the beginning of 2022 feeling zero self-worth to the point of not having a desire to continue my profound life's journey on earth. I am sensitive by nature, and after going through a recent divorce and facing many demons in such a short amount of time, a supervisor of mine started to reveal many of my insecurities, doubts, and fears, and this knocked me to the lowest point in my life.

I always knew I was meant to be a teacher. I was blessed to work at my kids' school, and I loved everyone I worked with, but I endured unprovoked judgment based mostly on my character as a single mom and a kind person. I was repeatedly told, "I am sure being a single mom makes it hard to be a teacher," and "The kids only listen to you because they like you." My skills and experience were constantly ridiculed with no evidence to base it on, and I was frequently punished for standing up for myself when I obviously knew I was being targeted.

After making the decision to leave in the middle of the school year, it left a dark, heavy hole in my heart that I can still feel when going through similar experiences of judgment from others. But, I also knew that if I continued under that leadership, I would never be good enough because my boss had honed in on me as the victim to her selfish, destructive nature of using people's weaknesses against them. And that's no longer on me. The things she said and did to me were absolutely cruel, uncalled for, and strategically malicious. Her double standards and continuous conflicting expectations led me to be more confused in my life than I have ever been.

After witnessing her behavior toward many of my coworkers and then later learning about many other innocent bystanders in her path, I realized this unfortunate experience was actually for a greater purpose revealed in my life's journey. I had to recognize that insecurities likely fueled her disdain for others, and I had to fully heal my insecurity, people-pleasing tendencies, and grow into someone who would stand up for those feeling silenced. I accepted that her behavior toward me was solely based on her own personal discomfort and avoidance in healing her pain, so I made the decision not to return to her venomous power trip and send a message that would put a stop to her vindictive behavior.

I hope my excruciating experience can help another victim escape a similar power hungry storm and send a message that love will always win over darkness. This is why it is so important that we all, regardless of our position in the world, accept our strengths and grow through our weaknesses while recognizing the tone we bring to our team. We have the power to see growth in ourselves even when others appear to see a different version. Everyone has a role to play in our life experiences, and it takes courage in knowing one self and being able to step away from a situation or a person who is only holding us back. I have actually come to accept gratitude in the lessons through the difficult experiences which bring hope in knowing my future challenges are opportunities for growth.

Now there's always another side of the coin when it comes to healthy, well-rounded self-help strategies. Interestingly enough, even though the recognition of who you are is important, it should not be a permanent instruction manual to our lives. It is through the continuous interactions and experiences that influence your life that defines different molds of who you are becoming during different stages of life. Our life's purpose is revealed before us in stages rather than one traumatic life-changing moment. If we stumble through life with a stubborn mentality of "that's just who I am and I won't change," then our connections with others will flounder rather than flourish.

Knowing who we presently are is not the prize at the end of a game. It's not the grand finale that causes everything in your life to suddenly fall into place. Rather than asking "Why should I continue to work on myself? I've already done the introspective work." we can recognize that our lives are ever-changing and, by keeping our head, heart, and feet in the present, we can continue to ask ourselves, "What can I do in this moment to live successfully? What do I presently have that will allow me to move forward with my goals? What can I work on to be a better version of myself tomorrow?"

We must place ourselves in the present and future rather than staying stuck in past versions of ourselves. Learning from the past will give more power and meaning to the present moments, which in turn catapults your future success in profound ways.

Connecting with Others Face-To-Face

Now that you've gotten to know yourself inside and out, you're in a better position to begin connecting with others outside of you. At first, this may feel a bit foreign as you step into a new version of yourself, but connecting with others face to face doesn't have to feel fake. As Nicholas Epley said in his book *Mindwise*, "If being transparent strengthens the social ties that make life worth living, and enables others to forgive our shortcomings, why not do it more often?" When we connect with others on a genuine level, it builds trust. And when people trust one another, they are more likely to be open and honest, creating a safe space where vulnerabilities can be shared and relationships can deepen.

Transparency is a beautiful thing. Trust is built on knowing someone so well that their actions and words become almost predictable. They are reliable, not quick to judge, and know so much about you and your vulnerable side that you can trust them with your words, during moments of disagreement, and can have faith in this connection. You can trust that they will build you up during your times of adversity and celebrate with you during your times of triumph. This is why I believe transparency and trust are vital aspects of connecting with others face to face. But true genuine connection like this only comes natural to us when we've built our own connection and trust within ourselves from a place of non-judgment. If you don't truly know who you are and what brings you passion in life, how do you expect to be transparent enough to build connections with others?

Now, on the flip side of things, while nourishing your true self and discovering your individual walk in life, it's key to remember one important thing: the value in productively communicating and showing your loved ones who you are while also respecting who THEY are. It is easier said than done, but once you've taken the shift and identified what you want, what you are passionate about, and who you are, you will find it is much easier to respect others in their life journey. In order to live a purpose-driven life filled with genuine connections, we need to validate the importance of our loved ones' personal growth. Do not get so lost in finding yourself that you lose sight of those around you! We must be continuously looking out for each other with check-ins, healthy disagreement, productive advice, and intentional face to face interactions.

With the COVID 2020 epidemic, so much was being done online. Interviews, family time, teaching, even exercise classes! While connecting during this time may start online and through phone conversations, our true colors shine in person. I vividly remember meeting with my sister during quarantine. The time in my life when I was faced with the divorce process. We met along a random creek outside of the city. Laughing, joking, serious conversations, even arguing about our opinion of the current situation we were faced with, this was a very important experience for me during this challenging time. It was a face to face connection that we both needed in order to remind us what's important in life. Why going through a hard time together with the disagreements along with the exchange of laughter was so important IN PERSON!

Being able to truly trust another person with your deepest thoughts and experiences is so important. Accepting each other for our quirks, disagreements, missteps, and even our rough past trauma and decisions is what connecting should be about. We may not have always agreed that night, but she truly listened to me and saw me for exactly who I am without a filter. She unconditionally cared for what I was faced with and for the mistakes I was making along the way. The location didn't matter, what I was wearing didn't matter, my problems and stressors didn't matter. What mattered was that I was physically present with my sister. The person who has seen every side of me throughout my entire life.

Connecting with Others at Work

As far as connecting with others in our career, in-person connection will always have an important role. Have you ever been hired for a position in your career without meeting your supervisor and/or colleagues in person? If so, then you likely understand why we must develop the skills to make good connections with people IN PERSON! Even though many jobs currently hold most meetings online, having the opportunity to meet in person usually brings a greater sense of feeling seen and heard. There's a certain energy exchange that occurs when we meet in person, regardless of any nervousness or tension that might be present. Human connection is what makes the world turn.

I believe there are two key factors that influence a first impression for a job: trust and competency. With the social media world we currently live in, many supervisors are able to click and view who you portray yourself as via social media without even meeting you in person! They can google your past, your work experience, and even sometimes where you have lived. The ultimate factor that influences their decision to hire you is if you can be trusted with others. No one wants to hire someone who can't relate with and connect with other people within the workplace. Portraying your professional image is very important in your career. I fear that this new-aged social media generation will lose sight of a confident, physical presence that can be professionally trusted. Work ethic is a skill that is learned with experience.

When it comes to personal connections, we can usually be our unadulterated selves, but in the workplace, there is indeed a difference. Being able to decipher this difference can be challenging. I find myself a bit torn when deciding between who I truly want to be at work and who I am "supposed to be." I am a teacher who has a very important audience. My students see me as an influential role model in their lives, and I know this is something I must take very seriously. My social media account does not always portray a bright, perfect image of a teacher. I'm vulnerable, honest, controversial at times, and don't always fit into the status quo in life. I am a single mom of three young kids who enjoys my free time with my friends who are not teachers. I have enjoyed dating and connecting with others outside of work. I am a "work in progress" when it comes to my career.

This is where I must notice my unique ability to see people for who they truly are. My professionalism is not always customary to what my boss might want to see. I'm honest, I speak the truth even when no one else will, and I try very hard to fight for what's right in the world of education. I see what's of value for my students, so I tend to go against the grain when it comes to the mentality of conforming and doing things to satisfy the people above us. Even though this might not always "fit" in the current education world, I still have faith that speaking truth that benefits those without a voice is always important regardless of the discomfort it might bring others. Discomfort in hearing the truth should spark change rather than avoidance.

I know my purpose in teaching is educating the future and taking care of my students in ways others can't always see. I see each of them as individuals along their own path to self-discovery and connection with others. I am truly blessed to have a career I am passionate about. Even though the political aspect of education will always be present, I will always do right by my students. I have a strong work ethic and a desire to be successful at any position I hold, but I have always felt different. I believe we are all placed in the right place at the right time to influence and connect with the very people we work with. Do you value your influence and leadership in your current job? Do you feel invisible and unheard day after day? How can you rise up to your true purpose in your career while also being mindful in respecting professionalism and the conflicting beliefs of others?

Now, there will ALWAYS be people who straight up don't like you. This is just a harsh part of life. The thing we must remember, especially those of us with a sensitive nature like myself, is that there is no pressure to force a connection. I find this very true at work. We need to recognize our personal power in deciding when it's time to move onto something different in our career and grow from both the negative and positive connections and experiences in order to nourish the connections that matter most to us. The relationships that add value to our lives. Not just to our careers.

While I was working at the front desk at a very well-known gym in Boston, our supervisors started incentivizing employees with "points" when they interact with members of the club. Before this was a thing, I genuinely interacted and knew almost every person that walked through the front door. I admired their perseverance to create a predictable workout regimen, and the people I would see walk through that door at the same time each day became a predictable part of my routine. They knew me and I knew them. I became the familiar face on Tuesday and Thursday mornings, and many of the members took the time to get to know me as a person. When I broke my ankle and was on a knee scooter, people genuinely cared to know what happened and how they could help. One of the girls I worked with actually started bringing my daily coffee to the front desk so I wouldn't have to go to the cafe.

People are good. We are social, caring creatures. Should caring and connecting be rewarded, or should we nurture our natural desire to develop connections with the people we see every day? It was quite funny to me, but I did work with a generation of social media/tech experts. The ones who needed to learn the true art of connecting with people through practice. It's a scary fact that this natural desire to connect with people we see on a day to day basis is disappearing. That it might need to be rewarded rather than instinctively done. How can we change this? How can you help someone see the true value of face to face connection today?

Another instance when I struggled to understand the value and purpose of connection was during my time working in multilevel marketing. The connections associated with this company geared toward natural healing and a healthy lifestyle, which felt like a deeply purposeful calling of mine. Because I was selling a product, I was afraid people would think my efforts at connecting were only for the ulterior motive of sales. Even though I genuinely promoted my business as a platform toward the health and well-being of others, and I truly saw value in what I was selling, I still felt fear that my motive to sell would push people away. I felt successful in this business for a time, but I also felt that my fear of what others thought caused me to fail. People know and see what we're about. We can usually sense passion and know what true connection feels like behind someone's motive. I have learned that when our intentions are pure, people see value in spending their hard-earned money to support our endeavors.

I still use all the products from this company and even still have income as a result of others finding value in the products. I made some wonderful connections and relationships within this company and often wonder how successful this business opportunity could have been if I would have removed the fear of being told no and being judged. I questioned my influence on others, and this was my demise.

How are you portraying yourself today? Are you influencing others in your career through positive interaction? Do you value the work you do and see your purpose at your daily job?

We often allow our egos to get in the way of truly connecting with others, and this also slows the natural progression in a relationship. It's better to drop the ego and occasionally be exposed rather than put on a front of always being perfect. Our role in our career is important and provides the financial needs necessary for survival in society. But are your connections at work and how people view you bringing true meaning in your greater purpose? Will these connections matter at the end of your life? Don't discredit your value and influence at work; however, don't allow the fear of failure and being exposed in the workplace cause personal setbacks. Work hard, play hard, and determine whether those connections matter enough to benefit your purpose in life. Being successful doesn't have to mean sacrificing your character or relationships. It's an amazing feeling to find success in your career and shine a positive light on those you spend much of your time with on a daily basis.

chapter

5

Comparison Trap - Fear and Doubt versus Love and Trust

What everyone else is doing is their business, and what you are currently doing is your business. It's as simple as that, right? Or is it? My mom always said, "Worry about yourself." So why should we seek feedback or observe others when making decisions or possibly changing our set patterns in life? It's as simple as this: true connection in our interactions can allow us to trust in others, while disconnection brings about fear and skepticism. Embracing and sharing our imperfections can not only enhance our personal connections but also create a more compassionate and understanding environment. Our flaws don't diminish our worth; rather they contribute to our humanity and relatability.

Having a bit of healthy competition in this way can provide growth within ourselves to become better, right? As long as we maintain our personal identity and don't stray from our life's purpose, comparison can be healthy and necessary to help us embark on the less conventional route that leads to new discoveries and a way of solving a problem. We are all diverse individuals who learn from others' experiences as well as our own, but we have to be wary of over-relying on the opinions and lives of others to dictate our next move.

I believe we spend too much time worried about making a decision or walking a certain path that others might not agree with. Sometimes it's freeing to go the more unconventional route in your life to reveal the mysteries and amazement of the road less traveled. It's scary, but don't we learn best through trial and error and experimentation? What if the great inventors, leaders, and revolutionary people in history hadn't made the decision to throw a wrench in what was considered normal and conventional in order to make massive shifts in our human history?

Never allow others to dictate your decisions. No matter how scary, unconventional, or plain crazy. We are all here for our own purpose and have our own God-given gut instincts to lead the way. At times in life, our ego will feel inferior, and we might become submissive. As a woman, I feel this comes up for us very often. In a world where the power of man is still the main driving force in most positions of power, women MUST be confident enough to hold our ground when necessary. That is why truly knowing who we are and what we stand for during vulnerable situations is vital. We have to recognize that although being a woman in this world is challenging, it is NOT a weakness. In retrospect, the feminine influence and impact on our future world is a powerful force that can be used to our advantage in any situation. It's a balance of both the masculine and feminine nature that can exist within everyone.

Dealing with Jealousy

So far, we've hashed out how true authentic connection can lead to a thriving life full of possibilities, and I've hinted at how harmful the comparison trap can be for us. So why shouldn't we all just transform into the person who always stays in their own lane without minding what everyone else around us is doing? Well, I say there's a time and a place. We must recognize when to put on our blinders and forget what everyone else is doing and when to take a huge piece of humble pie and receive constructive feedback from others.

Have you ever found yourself lying in bed at night reliving how the day went and what you could have said or done differently? Has this line of thought ever led to a sense of anxiety and fear that prevented you from sleeping? If you really stop and reflect on the core root of these thoughts and anxiety, most of the time it's usually a situation where you allow fear of judgment through comparison to take the wheel.

As a mother of three busy kids and a woman who works directly with many people on a daily basis, I experience fear of judgment and potential "foot in mouth" moments on a daily basis. In those moments, I have to tell myself that if my words and actions are rooted in love and care for someone, then I do not need to worry. That another person's response to the way I handle my day is not my problem. We all need to understand that it's often easier to point out what others are doing "wrong" rather than accept our own faults and work toward understanding and mutual respect. It's important to recognize that our fears and anxiety could be a result of worrying more about what others are doing wrong, which creates a negative cycle in avoiding growth and accountability. Our fears and anxieties are often influenced by external pressures and societal expectations. When everyone is preoccupied with pointing out others' mistakes or worrying about others' opinions, it can create a negative feedback loop. This environment can make it difficult for individuals to take ownership of their mistakes and grow from them. Understanding that these fears might stem from a broader, often unproductive cycle can be a crucial step in breaking free from it and fostering personal growth. It's important to focus on self-improvement and constructive feedback rather than getting caught up in the cycle of blame and fear.

As we discussed earlier, people who discriminate typically have their own personal burdens and figurative "walls" that they need to break down. So we should always try our best not to take criticism or a disagreement personally. And we must strive to not compare our lives to those we see around us. Our perception only shows a sliver of what someone else is dealing with. I truly believe that when people feel threatened or insecure, they tend to project their own discomfort onto others by focusing on others' perceived faults. This can be a defense mechanism to cope with their own feelings of inadequacy or envy. By highlighting others' weaknesses, they might be attempting to shift attention away from their own insecurities or diminish the perceived threat.

Understanding this dynamic can help you maintain a sense of confidence and resilience in the face of negativity. Instead of taking such reactions personally, we have to recognize them as reflections of the other person's struggles rather than a true assessment of our worth or abilities. This perspective can make it easier to navigate these interactions without being unduly affected by them.

Jealousy is often a fear response, while acceptance arises from trust. When we feel jealous, it creates a block in our ability to truly connect with others by not trusting their purpose in our lives. When we negatively compare ourselves to others, often from a place of inadequacy, jealousy will almost always rear its ugly head. This comparison can create a barrier, preventing us from fully engaging with and appreciating those around us.

It's our job to recognize this jealousy as a fear response and ask ourselves, "How can I use this emotion to effectively connect with people who may seem superior to myself?" We must transform a subtle feeling of jealousy into constructive growth rather than a negative trap because it can cloud our judgment and make it harder to see the positive aspects of relationships. It can lead to mistrust and hinder our ability to genuinely connect with others when we're more focused on our own insecurities and perceived shortcomings.

Recognizing jealousy for what it is—a reflection of our own internal struggles—can be a first step toward overcoming it. By working on self-acceptance and shifting our focus from comparison to celebrating others' successes, we can foster more meaningful and supportive connections. This shift not only benefits our relationships but also helps us grow personally and professionally.

I have personally learned that some of my common triggers when interacting with others often come when someone starts a sentence with "You can't. . .," "Why didn't you. . .," "Don't worry so much about. . .," and anything else that invalidates or misunderstands my emotions. I have learned that in order to prevent a triggered response that will only lead to either shutting someone out, offending them, or projecting my triggered feelings onto them, I have to explain my understanding in the situation. As I have always said, we all have different experiences and different personality traits that others are not always aware of. And while some people will lead a conversation pointing fingers at your faults simply to help you become better, there will come a time when someone is simply projecting their own insecurity onto you in order to feel more competent. Constructive criticism aims to help you grow and improve and is often delivered with the intention of support and guidance. However, when feedback comes from a place of personal insecurity or a need to elevate oneself over someone else, you can be sure they're more worried about their own issues rather than your actual shortcomings. While I find the latter to be an awful response, it's important to maintain our personal power and respond productively rather than reactively. It's so important that we listen and understand someone's point of view in order to learn and grow from each other rather than continue to spread bias and hate. We are all continuously learning from one another through our thoughts, feelings, and experiences. The comparison trap serves no one in this endeavor.

I like to handle uncomfortable situations like this by exposing my vulnerability right out of the gate either by sharing a story about a careless mistake I have made, like using stew meat from the freezer rather than strawberries when making a smoothie (yes, I have done that), or accidentally using powdered sugar instead of flour when making chicken fried steak. If we want people to trust us and feel comfortable enough to develop true, deep connections, we have to expose some of our weaknesses and even the adversity we've overcome so they feel comfortable rather than intimidated. Even though my silly stories didn't end with a tragic result (my friends liked to call it a "meat donut"), this simple example could help someone overcome a personal insecurity and accept that we all make mistakes. Sharing personal imperfection is one of the best methods of human connection.

Think about it, have you ever completely trusted someone when they only talk highly of themselves or pretend they have been perfectly on track in life without any mistakes or hardships? I sure haven't. I have always believed that by being candid, sincere, and humble, we can break the ice and help others feel more connected and secure in our interactions.

The Comparison Trap

Social media is a never-ending comparison trap. We have to learn to navigate the emotions that this generates and use the social media world to our advantage. I cannot imagine what this road will be like twenty years from now, but we must be prepared for the sake of humanity. Some people have the ability to block out the distractions, avoid the comparison traps, put on their blinders, and pour their full attention into a goal while ignoring anything else they perceive as "in their way." While this can result in quick results for some people, the true root of happiness is the connections we make along the way. The importance of being fully aware of how our actions and words can impact the people around us both online and in person. Especially those who matter most to us. It's truly about balance.

When navigating the comparison trap within face to face as well as digital connections, it's important to keep in mind where the source of comparison is coming from and identify potential feelings of jealousy or even reasons for changing your thoughts and ideas based on others' feedback or actions. Looking toward others for inspiration is powerful, but there are a few things you should keep in mind when you find yourself diving into the comparison trap:

- **Evaluate the Source:** Consider the relationship you have with the person you're comparing yourself to. Are they someone who genuinely wants to see you succeed, or is it from someone who might feel threatened or insecure?
- **Look for Constructive Elements:** Even if the feedback feels more like projection, try to extract any useful points. Sometimes, even negative feedback can contain nuggets of truth that can be beneficial.
- **Trust Your Self-Awareness:** Rely on your own sense of self-awareness and confidence. If you're aware of your strengths and areas for improvement, you can better discern whether the feedback is truly valuable or just a projection of someone else's insecurities.
- **Set Boundaries:** If the feedback feels hurtful or unhelpful, it's okay to set boundaries and distance yourself from overly critical or negative influences. Surrounding yourself with supportive, constructive people can foster a healthier environment for growth.

Discussing challenges and imperfections can open up conversations about personal growth and learning through experience. Having productive conversations while attempting to understand a different point of view can inspire others to reflect on their own experiences and growth journey. This often leads to meaningful dialogue and mutual support. Genuine connections through empathy, openness, and trust can help counteract fear and distrust, leading to more fulfilling and supportive relationships.

Emotion: The Good, The Bad, And The Ugly

As a sensitive soul who has experienced multiple traumatic events in my life, identifying and researching emotions has become a passion of mine. I have discovered that my experience with a wide spectrum of extreme emotions has allowed me to find gratitude and meaning behind every emotion I have felt, no matter how heavy it may feel. Believe it or not, your emotional intelligence can be connected with the amount of success you have in your overall life. Accepting all emotions, the good, bad, and the ugly, is the foundation of discovering yourself, living a life of resilience and true happiness, and building genuine connections with others.

Identifying and accepting your emotions equates to being able to thrive in all situations. Emotions are data that should never be completely ignored or swept under a rug. You can't hide from your emotions forever; they'll eventually make themselves known. It's about regulating them, learning to control them, and seeking the reason behind why they exist. My brother once told me rather than focusing on the pain that comes from the tough feelings, focus on being grateful that they exist. For without emotion, we would lack the depth to nurture profound connections.

Emotional experiences can vary from person to person. I even find that my personal states of happy, sad, frustration, and anger will vary to some degree on a daily basis depending on all aspects of my physical, emotional, and situational state of being. What has worked for me through experience is immediately recognizing and evaluating how I am feeling each day and giving myself grace.

The year 2024 brought many challenges, uncertainty, and situations that I felt were out of my control. Ironically, the word I chose for the year was warrior, and this word proved to be spot on through my experiences. My oldest son has autism, and his last year in middle school proved to be one of the most trying times for me as his advocate. An already tumultuous time for a teenager with autism navigating change, I felt like a warrior at battle trying to make sure he was putting his best foot forward while also getting the support he needed at school. I was also at war trying to determine how my backyard was flooding, financial burdens with the economy, my own personal medical issues, many challenges in my job, all while trying to juggle busy schedules. I was all too familiar with powering through pain, adversity, and ignoring the emotions standing in my way after everything I had been through in 2020. I powered on until I could no longer. I covered my mixed emotions with anger and resentment. I ignored the emotions until they were physically screaming at me. I felt like a fuse waiting to explode on any small disappointment.

One morning, I stopped at a Chick Fil A parking lot while on a work call and decided to place a mobile order for breakfast. When I went inside to quickly grab my order and continue powering through my busy day, I learned it wasn't ready. I had no choice but to mention it to the staff. All she had to say was, "Well, we have a problem," and I immediately broke down into uncontrollable tears. Breakfast was no longer being served. I remember the confused way she looked at me for crying over a breakfast burrito.

"It's okay, it's not the food, I will just go," I said.

And she graciously replied, "Honey, please let me get you something else since you paid."

I agreed and immediately fled in embarrassment and sat down on the curb outside the restaurant waiting for a new order, publicly sobbing through all the disappointment, anger, and heaviness that I had ignored for too long until it all publicly exploded. All these repressed emotions, combined with a sense of embarrassment, failure, and pain throughout my body that had finally released after being stuffed down for too long. A kind stranger approached me and asked, "What can I do?" and I said, "Pray for me," and she sat there on the curb in front of Chick fil A, embraced me, and prayed for healing over me. I thanked her and gave her the biggest hug, letting her know that her kind gesture meant more to me than I could ever explain.

When I went back in for my food, the kind lady who initially saw me break down handed me a bag of food and said, "I stuck some chocolate chip cookies in there for you, honey. Things will only get better for you." While I don't recommend allowing your emotions to get so repressed that you end up breaking down in a fast food restaurant, this simple act of kindness changed the entire day for me. I walked in the faith that everything would work out. I later decided to share my story on a community social media page, and it brought immense attention and comments of similar experience and heart-warming gratitude for the power of human kindness. It's so important to recognize how simple gestures, words, and actions can shift someone's mood or even life.

I think we can all agree that life is not consistently smooth sailing. There is not one person who is invincible to sorrow and misfortune. Bad things happen to everyone, and when we all have a certain expectation of what life should be like, some of the challenges seem to knock us down all at once, flooding us with overwhelming emotions. When things don't go exactly as planned, our instinctive reaction can be to sulk, repress our emotions with unhealthy distractions, or even become rebellious or give up. Our road maps in life can sometimes lead us astray with numerous curve balls that often cause our attempts at success to appear to fall short. Of course, this often brings up the not-so warm and fuzzy emotions, and without healthy coping strategies, this can lead to unhealthy behavior patterns or unnecessary stress.

While we are all guilty of throwing ourselves a pity party or indulging in guilty pleasures in order to numb the ugly emotions, these bad habits can turn into repetitious cycles that are hard to break. And poor habits are often followed by clouded judgment and a lack of motivation in life. Repetitive use of negative coping strategies, such as avoidance, procrastination, or substance abuse, reinforces these habits over time. They become default responses to stress, making them harder to change. When we're caught in a cycle of negative coping, our ability to make clear and rational decisions can be compromised. It can easily become a downward spiral if those underlying emotions are not recognized and handled properly.

One strategy for handling these tough emotions is to genuinely feel them. While this may sound simple, we humans try very hard to avoid tough emotions. The negative thought patterns such as "Bad things always happen to me. Why do I even bother? " or "Why can't my life be as easy as everyone else's?" are prime examples of not feeling and accepting the tough emotions. The more we practice identifying the emotion and expressing the feelings in productive ways, the more we will improve our ability to handle them.

I often find myself referring back to my own reflection questions from chapter 1 to reflect, journal, and decide to avoid negative coping or allowing my emotions to become too heavy. Set a daily timer and spend five minutes at the beginning and the end of the day in quiet surrender or put on a good song, stare at the wall, and make a decision to feel any emotions that come up! You would be surprised how much better sleep you can get if you can sit, accept the emotions coming in, and feel the power in deciding why and what you might need the next day. Whether your emotions need soothing through a hot cup of tea, a bath, a walk outside, the gym, or a phone call with a loved one, silencing the noise for a brief time and allowing yourself to feel your emotions will soothe your mind, body, and soul and set you up for success through self-love and self-care.

After spending time alone feeling the emotions and validating why they exist, we are better equipped to handle the day with grace and understanding. This proactive recognition within yourself will reduce reactive behaviors and responses that could potentially cause damage in your daily interactions. While crying in front of others or alone can bring discomfort or potential embarrassment and can appear as a weakness to some, it can actually be a form of pressure release in the body. As social creatures, we instinctively want to help or soothe another person we see crying.

This social response not only releases the powerful, healing hormone of oxytocin for the person crying but also in the person recognizing their need for attention and acceptance through soothing! It is truly a win win! While I understand that not everyone is comfortable crying, we must recognize that crying is a form of communication rather than a weakness. As I said earlier, someone else's judgment and thoughts on crying as an emotional response is not our burden to carry. I truly believe when someone is publicly crying, they have either held it together long enough that it was not by choice, or it might be a literal cry for help.

I will fully admit that I will sometimes cry regardless of who is around, and this is usually more so when I have not spent time really caring for myself. Shedding a few tears won't usually draw undesired attention, but my "ugly cry" experience can show up without warning when I have been avoiding self-care for too long. When someone is being vulnerable enough to cry, there is underlying hurt and pain that we might not see. And while we wouldn't want to spend most of our lives crying profusely and being inconsolable, as my story from earlier shows, I truly think crying can be a healthy way to connect with others as well as ourselves on a deeper level. Sadness can actually be an emotion that is required on the other side of feeling angry, disappointed, abandoned, or fearful. Journaling or even talking to someone you trust can lead to the understanding that sadness is a release of false expectation and pressure to be perfect and happy all the time. No matter your belief in the social acceptance within crying, we all need to understand that some of us experience unexpected crying as a form of release.

Everyone has experienced their own versions of trauma that they carry day in and day out. Small moments can offer the opportunity to surrender to the painful emotions rather than toying with them and allowing them to control us. We actually have the ability and power to control them. When going through some of the hardest times in our lives, recognizing the uncomfortable emotions and coping that has worked in the past might not be as effective. Sitting in the tough emotions with acceptance in knowing it's painful and giving yourself the time to heal is actually profound power. I believe that the darkest times in my life have paved the path to my own self-realization.

Unfortunately for me, powering through life's traumatic experiences, attempting to ignore the uncomfortable emotions because I felt something was "wrong with me," and distracting myself in the "busy" actually prolonged my personal healing many times in my life. By understanding vulnerability through your hardships, it allows us to take an objective view of our thoughts and emotions. Rather than feeling defeated and creating negative judgment in my emotions, I try to find more time to observe and seek appreciation and gratitude for the simple pleasures that bring joy through the difficult times. Constant comfort zones won't always ignite gratitude. It's the tough chapters in life that incite reflection of who we authentically are and eventually lead us to making the boldest moves toward our life's true purpose and strongest connections.

Conflict with Our Emotions

It's important to recognize emotions while not initiating conflict with them. The negative feelings we experience are like gray clouds passing by for a moment. When we make the choice to provoke these feelings and allow them to take over our identity, the gray clouds turn into a nasty thunderstorm that we are then forced to endure. This usually leads to further negative feelings such as remorse, exhaustion, depression, or anxiety. Our emotions are just like any other bodily sense or sensation: temporary. Think about it, Did something make you angry last month, last week, or yesterday? Are you still angry about it today? Most likely not. And if you are, it's likely not the same level of anger that it once was. With time and introspection, our emotions are able to shift and change effortlessly. It is so important to train your mind to recognize emotion, reflect on and own your response, and take control before your emotions take control over you.

My personality can often encompass multiple extremes, and even though this may sound like a weakness, I realize through self-reflection that I often used my overly friendly nature and desire to genuinely connect with people to both break down their barriers and hide my insecurity. I realized I might sometimes come across as fake or "too friendly," which can be a huge turn off for some people. I spent so much of my life feeling so much pressure to form relationships and get people to like me that I lost sight of who I was and what I was passionate about. My phobia of being disliked inhibited my ability to show my creative self. I would often avoid voicing my opinion at the expense of appearing extra outgoing or friendly. I spent far too much time worrying about something that I was actually really good at: connecting with people! Through recognizing when and why my neurotic nature would come up as a sign rather than a weakness, I was able to use it to my advantage and even steer my life toward a more calm and accepting version of myself.

When you become emotional, try to name the emotion, identify what it is associated with, and understand why you could be feeling this way. Rather than placing blame on another person's words or actions, it's very important to understand the purpose of the emotion that is coming up for you. This will create a much more balanced approach at handling conflict.

Dealing with Triggers

If someone is vulnerable enough to explain how they feel and why, it's important to avoid justifying your actions or gaslighting the other person for any past behaviors because this would just invalidate their feelings and present more conflict. Even when someone says something that appears offensive or opposite to what you meant, it's key to understand both sides rather than defending what you did. If the conversation becomes more heated, we can have the power to hear, understand, and respond in more productive ways. When we have awareness of our emotions and how we can respond when they come up rather than being controlled by them, we can achieve the most powerful potential in any situation and gain full control of our life.

While emotions can be valid, this doesn't necessarily mean throwing in the towel and completely losing our shit without remorse anytime we feel negative emotions. It's about learning your individual triggers and getting ahead before they get the best of you. Because let's be honest, most of us have experienced a time or two where we allowed our emotions to take full control and not respond in the healthiest manner. It's about learning from those times. It's knowing what you are in control of and what you can't control and letting go of the desire for complete control in all situations. It's simply recognizing that emotions come and go, and we as humans are continuously a work in progress, transforming into an adaptable person who can productively collect ourselves when necessary. It's a beautiful thing when you can appreciate this natural mechanism and tool known as emotions and have an ability to tame the dragon before it's able to cause destruction. A few triggers to consider prior to allowing them to take over:

- **Words directed toward you**: As I said earlier, times when people start a sentence with "You need to," "You should," or "You can't" will usually stir something within me. When these words come from someone I am close with, I can address the way it stirs me up and have a conversation built in trust and love. But when they come from someone I don't know as well, I understand that this person is probably confident in their advice without considering how it comes across, so it's easy for me to let go or grow through this type of advice.

- **Feeling like our kids or even ourselves are not treated equally:** Facing adversity within situations that seem unfair can stir up a lot of internal pain and push me into a state of defense mode. When it comes to my kids, the "momma bear" within me will start rattling the cage, and I have had moments where I said something I later regret. I have had many moments where I almost grabbed my kids in the middle of an uncomfortable situation and sent a nasty gesture on our way out as a public display of frustration. But I have trained my mind to let my kids handle and respond to the situation on their own. My daughter had a raw moment of adversity during a volleyball game and responded by leaving the gym in tears. When I went out to check on her, I told her we could leave, but she said no. Someone came out to encourage her to give it another shot, I allowed momma bear to "slightly come out," in order to speak up from my daughter, which led to her saying, "I am ok now, I'm going back in,"

During most of my life, feelings were difficult to navigate. I had experienced so many times when I tried to express a negative feeling, and it was almost always followed by guilt within myself. There was always a sense of being "wrong" for feeling or talking about something on a deeper level. I really believe most of my generation was raised to sweep negative feelings under the rug and pretend they weren't there because bad feelings were seen as a weakness rather than a learning experience. I have learned for myself that if I need to discuss a problem I am having with someone, intense justifying of their actions or complete shut down through avoidance will not be tolerated from me. I speak this truth to my most cherished people. I own up to my mistakes to a fault, and I have spent years trying to "fix myself" with a false impression that something is wrong if I'm the only one feeling like there was a problem in communication. I carried far too much blame for simply feeling, and I had to discover the art in setting boundaries and validating my feelings.

Still to this day, even the smallest problem in my life suddenly feels like "my fault," so I have had to really build my emotional intelligence to understand the difference between something I can control and something that is in another's person's court. In order to handle our emotions and take responsibility for ourselves in uncomfortable situations, we must see emotions as an indicator of growth and lessons through experience.

Every human on the planet experiences negative emotions. Whether self-doubt, failure, insecurity, grief, heartbreak, disappointment, and even rock bottom hopelessness. It's ok to seek professional help during these challenging times. This is actually a method of evolving and taking your power back in life. The future generation is counting on us to be educated in handling our emotions before they take over. Too many tragic situations are taking place as a result of greed, jealousy, and anger tied into an inability to validate these feelings and handle them constructively. Self-management of emotions is an important skill to teach young adults.

If you are a sensitive soul who deeply feels your emotions but also picks up on the emotions of others, do not allow this sensitive nature to bring about a fear of failure or being misunderstood. Rather, know that you are one of the rare people with a gift of being able to feel deeply, and find purpose and understanding of these emotions on a higher level. Sensitive personality types must learn how to recognize our energy and feelings versus others, reflect on this input, and then react accordingly rather than take on what is not ours to begin with.

A friend recently gave me the best analogy of a swing. If you are like me and find yourself experiencing very high highs and extremely low lows, consider when you're on a swing and are going very high only to find yourself coming back even faster and further. Visualize yourself simply sitting on the swing rather than pushing back and forth.

Find your sense of equilibrium in daily life and journal the moments that you experience a sense of calm. Stay in this space and breathe through the moments when your emotions attempt to take over. Finding our emotional serenity through life's ups and downs is freeing and can bring an empowering sense of control through any situation.

Vulnerability

We all have personal baggage that we've been carrying around throughout our lives. Even as children, most of us had experiences that caused us to develop an insecurity or coping mechanism to protect our ego. No one has gone through life without experiencing at least one vulnerable moment, whether minor or extreme. It's truly what creates empathy and growth. The human mind is a mysterious thing.

Have you ever had a dream and woke up with a vivid recall of many details, thinking to yourself, "Where did that come from? I haven't thought about that person for so long, so why would they appear in my dream?" The subconscious mind can lock away our past traumas and even moments of triumph within our amygdala. This is why it's so important that we know and accept our past trauma so when a memory or experience causes us to feel out of control, we can recognize the uncomfortable emotions, understand how they were triggered, and be prepared with healthy coping mechanisms to handle these surfacing emotions. We must get vulnerable with ourselves before we can do it with others.

We need to recognize the difference between people unknowingly triggering a past trauma and when they intentionally use it as a weapon against us. Unfortunately for many narcissists, this is a common tactic used to make people feel weak and in need of someone to "save them." With this knowledge, you have the power to understand that most personal attacks from others are a reflection of their own inner conflict and pain, and it's necessary to pick and choose who you are vulnerable with. Not everyone deserves to see that side of you.

We often associate vulnerability with our interactions with others or specific situations. Whether it's bringing up an uncomfortable conversation in a relationship, asking for a promotion, achieving a long-term dream, interviewing for a top position in a company, or taking any extreme chances in your own life experience. But being vulnerable can also mean separating yourself and being completely alone. Fully willing to self-reflect and heal with no one else involved. I can tell you from personal experience of feeling painfully alone that connectedness does not always have to be from an outside source. Something powerful happens within you when you're completely alone. Unable to relate with another person. Unable to even disagree.

During my most excruciating times of loneliness, I had no choice but to find inner strength and wisdom to embody my personal ability to persevere. The hardest emotions are not always meant to be felt alone, but when faced with a time when you have no choice but to reflect alone because no one else seems to understand or can pull you through it, I found that this is a true indicator of soul purpose healing and a sign that I was meant for greatness. I knew that the figurative dark holes I would fall into would only bring the brightest of light on the other side.

We cannot always pick and choose who can "handle our darkness," so we must take responsibility for ourselves and pull ourselves back up, give ourselves more grace, and know that coming out on the other side will bring more strength even when we feel weak. However, seeking help and being vulnerable with someone should never be seen as a sign of weakness. I remember a specific moment in my life when I had no choice but to be vulnerable and share how heavy and overwhelming life had become. It was 2020—I was in the grocery store, trying to suppress the pain from a divorce, moving into a new house, starting a new job, and navigating the entire COVID pandemic. I decided to call my dad to check in, and before I knew it, I was in full-blown tears, standing in the middle of the store.

"I hate feeling this much! It's too heavy, and I don't know how to move forward when I have three kids relying on me to make this work—to pay the bills, get through the pain, and learn to lean on myself. I wish I could just turn off all the emotions and feel stronger," I told him.

What my dad said next will forever resonate with my purpose: "Feeling everything is who you are and why you're so important. We can't have everyone walking around pretending everything is okay without truly feeling and understanding how to make it better. That's what makes you special."

Loneliness can serve a purpose for self-discovery. Being alone led me to believe the true meaning of life is to connect and interact. I learned that strong relationships are rare. I learned that there is a time to stay in your lane without interrupting others' lives, and that being selfish serves a purpose at times. We all have our own life to live and it's vital to understand we will always have our individual selves to rely on. This is the relationship we should work to cultivate first: our relationship with self.

Loneliness should never be long-term and actually can't be sustainable; however, if we are able to rest in the comfort of being alone, not only will we grow as an individual, but we will become better equipped to assist others during their times of loneliness.

As I mentioned in the beginning of the book, not having my children at home with me can put me into a state of paralysis. When they are with their father, my role as a mother is swept right under my feet, and this has forced me to work really hard on being comfortable with being alone for days at a time. Being alone can feel natural for many people, but for someone like me who has never lived alone, this can be excruciating.

For those of you who can relate, becoming vulnerable and accepting myself, flaws and all, was a very painful road. It was during this time of being alone that I came to realize that I often used "people-pleasing" as a self-fulfilling tool that provided me with a sort of satisfaction in achieving "my life's purpose." The difficult times in my life forced me to take a hard look in the mirror and realize that I was so busy people-pleasing that I forgot to care for myself! I had always envisioned myself impressing others to such an extreme that they would want me around more often. Whether it was trying to achieve a "best friend" title, getting invited to the "popular kids" parties, having a boyfriend who adored me, or just being recognized by others, this was actually a trait I had developed as a result of fear. A fear of abandonment that I had developed early in my life. A fear of owning up to my own self-reflection after being haunted by so many self-sabotaging thoughts that I needed to shift. And it was because I had taken the time to be vulnerable with myself that I was able to have these realizations.

This realization of my false sense of "purpose" in life actually led me to reveal my inner childhood wound of abandonment and my attachment style. Having spent most of my life seeking approval from others rather than from myself, I had, in a way, neglected my inner child by constantly chasing external validation. Typically, people with "abandonment issues" can fall under either the "anxious attachment" personality, which is where I lie, or the "avoidant attachment." By giving yourself an opportunity to spend time alone without relying on anyone else as a distraction or someone to "fill the void," there is such potential in discovering your deep-seated pain and learning more about yourself than you ever knew before. While this is not the most utopian experience, as I've already discussed in this book, knowing who you are and recognizing where you need to heal is vital for all your connections to thrive.

While it's important to see value in all our relationships with others, we can't possibly be fully present and pour into our most important connections if we don't recognize our own great potential and ability to grow. Get comfortable in your own skin. Discover your biggest fears in life and get to the bottom of why they bring such discomfort and what could have led to them. The other side of fear is love, so learn to love yourself entirely and everything else will flow smoothly.

Something profound happens when we experience our mentally and physically weakest moments. The external things we often use to mask our problems, whether it's alcohol, caffeine, or food will no longer serve as a positive solution because your body WILL start to show the symptoms, red flags shouting, "I need nourishment, concern, and healing!" In these moments, our emotions demand to be recognized and dealt with rather than numbed away; otherwise, our physical body will speak up and it won't be pretty. Vulnerability opens a door to deep inner connection that we are rarely taught to tap into as children.

As I said before, in this social media era, imperfection is often not accepted, and perfection, though we know it is unattainable, is the goal. But with real, genuine human connections, we have to be able to put down our guard and share our deepest thoughts and struggles in order to gain trust, happiness, and form deep relationships. It's where the magic happens. It's OK to occasionally be wrong AND admit it! It's NOT ok to make excuses and continue with the same pattern of poor choices in an attempt to avoid accountability. Facing our faults and mishaps right smack dab in the face can be the most humbling spiritual awakening that we need to avoid being stagnant in the world.

In the throes of my loneliness, I knew all the steps to a healthy lifestyle. I inundated myself with information about supplements, physiology, and biology, and gut intolerances. The solutions seemed simple, but practicing them can sometimes be close to impossible if you aren't vulnerable with yourself and give yourself grace. My internal negative self-talk was toxic, coming up with constant excuses for why I wasn't successful in my goals rather than owning my faults and making a change on the inside as well as the outside. Something has to change internally in order to make a change externally.

I believe disease and illness start from emotional disconnection within ourselves that, when ignored, transforms into something that can no longer be ignored. If you're not handling your emotions, your physical body will let you know. So how can you own up to the excuses and shut out the noise of what my friend Kelley often calls the "itty-bitty shitty committee" that exists in your thoughts on a daily basis? We must face our fear and weaknesses. That's where the beauty lies. What can you do today that can lead to an internal and external shift to greatness in your life?

Life has a way of throwing obstacles in the most unexpected and yet opportune times. Being the vulnerable person in a situation humbles you and creates empathy. This is so important in the world we currently live in. We desperately need more empathetic people now more than ever. Empathy leads to positive change that benefits everyone.

Romantic Relationships

I know it's been said a million different ways, but it's so important to start this chapter by reiterating the importance of knowing what matters most in your personal life and fully understanding the values that you hold true in your own life. We have to know our personal "deal breakers" when it comes to life decisions before committing to any long-term relationship, romantic, platonic, or otherwise. Self-awareness is gold in any relationship! Of course we all change and grow as individuals over the years. But having the ability to grow and adapt with your forever relationship is so important. Here are some ideas for keeping your most important connection alive while also keeping yourself in check.

Sometimes it's safest to stay in your lane in order to protect your marriage or your relationship with your partner. The grass may sometimes appear greener on the other side, but the comparison trap can be volatile when it comes to relationships. This is why we continuously need to pour into and allow ourselves to be poured into by our significant others. This allows our personal relationships to blossom into a beautiful lifelong commitment.

I truly believe that every person we connect with is brought into our lives by God at the right time and for the right reason. Whether it was an unpleasant experience or a very positive transformative connection, we need to recognize that everyone has a purpose in our lives. And we also need to respect and nourish the reasons we are placed in other people's lives. It's really a magnificent thing when we recognize and reflect on every person and their purpose in our ever-changing lives. Even when these relationships have an expiration date.

Relationships should be seen as an intricate jeweled necklace. They take time to create and must have a strong foundation (the chain) that holds together every piece so it doesn't break and fall apart. Each bead is a unique facet of your past, present, and future that, when placed correctly, will create a gorgeous masterpiece. Sometimes this necklace can become tangled and requires tedious, intentional work to repair. Other times, if handled with care and even with some imperfections that have formed along the way, it will still be honored and appreciated forever and be seen as a beautifully designed treasure. If not handled with care, it might become knotted and ratted and could transform into a nuisance that no longer benefits but rather causes tension and frustration in our life. This disjointed relationship can easily cause all of our other relationships to suffer and then the ability to connect with others becomes almost impossible. We can only live in an unhealthy romantic relationship for so long before it starts negatively impacting our other relationships.

For instance, if you are in a relationship with someone who doesn't understand and own their true identity, you might continuously run into dead ends when trying to reason with them and be understood. If the people we interact with on a daily basis whether it be work colleagues, clients, family members, friends, or our partner are not seeking improvement or trying to reflect on growing in their own selves, they just won't be receptive to our suggestions and advice. Sometimes people just seek to be heard and understood rather than wanting a solution, so it's important not to take it personally or attempt "controlling" their thoughts and actions. Relating to them can be as simple as sharing your own personal experience while removing the need to change their mind because if they aren't willing to change or take action, then we can't expect them to take our advice. Many times, people just need a space where they can express themselves, share their thoughts, or vent without feeling the pressure to "fix" things. Simply being listened to, with empathy and without judgment, can provide a sense of relief and validation. It's a reminder that emotional support and understanding can be just as powerful as offering solutions. Sometimes, the act of being heard itself can bring clarity and comfort, even if no immediate solution is provided.

Toward the end of my marriage, it was a constant dead end with any discussion we had. For so much of our relationship, I had followed anything he desired in life as the path we followed, and this sometimes meant picking up our lives and moving across the country or even across the world. He worked long hours and was away from our family while traveling for long periods of time which led to us growing apart.

During this time, I worked on discovering who I was. When I decided to voice my thoughts on the lifestyle we were currently living and how I didn't know who he was anymore, it was always met with conflict. It turned into a blame game filled with gaslighting one another as "at fault," or victim to our lack in communication when in reality, we had both failed at growing together in mutual respect and understanding. My sense of abandonment and feeling misunderstood had to be deflected through avoidant "silent treatment," or else it would turn into an ugly argument. I felt completely out of his life because work was his full concentration and even when he called home while traveling, I would hand the phone to our kids having nothing to say that wouldn't lead to an argument.

A sense of abandonment is one of the most toxic feelings in a relationship. If not dealt with and recognized by the person choosing another distraction every day, it builds resentment and even distrust. Trust in a relationship is vital. It's like the veins that carry blood throughout our bodies. Once trust is broken, all aspects of the relationship are at risk. And oftentimes, it can be hard to regain trust. I always say, even though it can be extremely difficult, honesty is the best policy. Those tough conversations need to happen so the trust keeps flowing and the relationship thrives. Without trust, there is constant worry and discomfort which puts stress on a relationship.

I knew my romantic relationship had ended with my husband regardless of the fact that we had so much history and had created a family together. No one should be treated like a doormat that is only needed when it's convenient and fits into their personal goals and desires in life. In a marriage, it's a compromise of give and take in every situation, and we have to keep our most important relationships as a priority when making life-changing decisions. If one person spends most of the time sacrificing and agreeing to the other and allowing them to become consumed with work, it will almost certainly create resentment and distrust and a disconnected marriage.

Toward the end of my marriage, I had a friend tell me I should just "fake it 'til you make it" in my marriage. For whatever reason, this statement regarding my almost fourteen-year marriage stunned me. It took me a few days to realize why. In life, our most important connections should never be fake. Isn't this why we exchange vows "through sickness and in health, through good times and bad, for as long as we both shall live"? Why would I want to spend another moment pretending like the most important relationship in my life is solid when it's the most volatile, unstable relationship I had? Both you and your life partner should feel safe and comfortable with sharing your most vulnerable and honest sides without fear of it being used against you or being disregarded.

The trust in my marriage was broken, and the words that were said damaged both our vulnerable parts. We were no longer able to trust each other with our burdens because, for me, my most vulnerable time in life had been used as a weapon against me. In my opinion, the statement, "fake it 'til you make it" should only be applicable for relationships that are important in our careers or extended family. Definitely not our marriages.

When going through a rough patch in your marriage, one of the hardest things to decipher is when to know it's time to move on and when to fight the fight because you know the relationship is worth salvaging. Even when you know it's going to be one of the hardest things you go through, how do you know it's time to make the tough decision? Is there a profound moment when it's clear, even without definite infidelity, abuse, or abandonment? Well, from my experience, it's when you feel more like yourself when they aren't around. It's feeling so grounded and independent in your everyday life without them that you almost forget who you are when you are with them. When the day to day feels complete without them. It's when you've given your all and exposed all the sides of yourself to this person only to find the same patterns in their behavior continue to stunt your own growth in life. And while these feelings and signs certainly don't show up overnight, you will know when you're at the end of your rope, and it's time to make the tough call.

They say hindsight is 20/20, and unfortunately, many of us spend too much time regretting our decisions, unable to see the full picture sooner. Well, I have learned to accept that God does this for many reasons. There is true purpose behind every relationship, the good and the bad, and without my marriage, I would not have my three children. They are my life, and God knew that my soul would not be complete without them. My husband and I married for the hard lessons, and we married to procreate the wonderful humans that I get to call my own. They have a God-given purpose on this earth, and thankfully I was able to see when my romantic relationship with their father had run its course and when it was time for me to break free. We still cherish many precious memories from the early days of our relationship and continue to create a new version of it, one that benefits our children.

Even when I remember "the signs" that he and I would never work, I realize that the clarity I am currently experiencing could not have happened prior to this moment. That this realization of my failed relationship with the father of my children was inevitable, yet we needed to give it our best efforts. This is actually a gift that I can hold on to during this extremely difficult time of divorce in which I have questioned my decisions to move forward with. This sudden clarity of our failed relationship confirms to me that even though this decision is not easy, it is something that has been a long time coming. It's the moment that I take the road less traveled and endure the challenges so that he and I and even our children can start living a more meaningful, purpose-driven life.

One thing I will say about divorce and break-ups is that it can be terribly difficult. When you've spent a large part of your life with someone else, this sudden shift will bring up an enormous amount of emotion, uncertainty, and change. It can feel as if the rug has been swept right under your feet leaving you in a state of questioning everything. It's something that has left a deep wound that is still healing after being divorced for four years. I know so many people currently tempted in the idea of going through a divorce, but some things to consider in your present moment before making the decision are:

1. Make a list of the reasons you fell in love with your significant other. Come up with examples of how they still show these qualities and decide whether your needs have changed or whether they have changed as a person.
2. Remember that a relationship is not always 50/50. There will be days and even long stages throughout

a relationship where one person needs to pour more into the other. Consider how this has played out throughout your time with this person.

3. If you share children with this person, consider how coparenting will look if you decide to end things. While I do not believe in staying in a relationship solely for the kids, you have to consider the loss in control and needing to trust when your children are with the other person.

4. Come up with reflective questions for your partner. A few examples could be "How do you feel loved?" "What is currently bringing you joy in our life together?" "What are some things you need more of in your day?" They might not be able to answer right on the spot, but if they do then they have also been self-reflecting, which is a healthy start! If they appear stumped, allow them time to think about it and revisit it later. That opens the door to agreement in continuing the conversation while avoiding putting it off too long.

5. Be ready to own up to your feelings while also preparing yourself for their reaction. Try to set the tone for honesty while also respecting their thoughts and feelings. Discussing problems in a relationship can be very uncomfortable and even triggering for some people, so if you don't feel prepared for potential criticism or shared honesty with how they are feeling, suggest marriage counseling. Their response

to this suggestion will give you a good idea of whether they are also open to discussion or if they are completely blind-sighted by problems they haven't noticed.

Life Purpose

I was hesitant to write this final chapter because "Life Purpose" is viewed as an extremely valuable and self-fulfilling prophecy. Everyone aspires to live out their life purpose in some grand way. We were made to connect with others, understand and respect our differences, and refrain from overwhelming conflict. We have to recognize differences without judgment. Wouldn't you want to be that person for someone in their life? There's a glow that radiates when we feel accomplished in our relationships, careers, and health. And the root of all these very important aspects of our lives is emotional intelligence and true genuine connection.

We must navigate disagreements or conflict by recognizing and respecting that others may not have the same experiences and are, therefore, guided in their own personal understanding. We all want to be seen as valuable in others' lives and feel like we are living up to our full potential in our God-given gifts. Romans 12:2 states, "Do not conform to the patterns of this world but be transformed by the renewing of your mind." Rather than spend our lives achieving a grand purpose according to others' belief systems, we must allow ourselves to be transformed in our own learning and knowing on our walk in life. Transform all your experiences into positive opportunities to shift and grow into a better version of yourself.

It's ok to have moments in life when you feel broken or disconnected from others. That is where healing and profound reflections on who you are meant to be will happen. Don't allow the feelings of doubt, shame, or fear to consume you and sabotage your growth. In those moments of discomfort, determine where those negative feelings come from and understand that on the other side of those emotions lies growth, confidence, and love. By giving yourself grace and having a growth mindset rather than playing victim, you will evolve in self-love and that will reflect in all aspects of your life. Remind yourself that you are capable and worthy of greatness.

We are not meant to carry the weight of the world on our shoulders alone. No one is supposed to walk through life condescending their comrades or spending a majority of their time focused only on their feelings and selfish desires. We aren't meant to become materialistic and selfish in our ways. We are inherently codependent on one another, and we naturally crave human connection. No matter how different we all may be, we must accept that we are continuously learning from each other. In order to continue building an interconnected society, effective communication skills and valuable connections must be formed and nourished.

I see this journey of life as one we spend nourishing our most important relationships, knowing how to navigate through the tough times, forming connections with everyone around us all while truly recognizing the necessity for one another. It is so important to leave a positive impact on every person we interact with daily. No pressure-just genuine human connection. It's our job to let other people into our lives. I believe deep satisfaction and success will be the result for our future leaders, mothers, fathers, children, goal-seekers, and this will spread on a global scale. Shut out the noise and connect already. Identify and challenge any beliefs or narratives that are holding you back. Reframe your limiting beliefs into positive, empowering statements that support your growth and aspirations. Take ownership of your experiences and decisions rather than feeling controlled by external circumstances or past events. Treat yourself with kindness and understanding, especially when making changes or facing difficulties. Stay aligned with your core values and authentic self so you can navigate your life with intention and confidence. Surround yourself with people who support and encourage your growth.

You choose the narrative in your story. You have the right to fearlessly make changes, conscious choices, and use your personal power to shift and change your narrative to lead a more fulfilling and empowered life.

Note from the Author

I'm so grateful that you decided to embark on the journey to Shut Out the Noise and Connect Already! My vision was to offer heartfelt guidance and encouragement helping you recognize the opportunity to discover the most amazing version of yourself—no matter the noise around you. Writing has always been my outlet, especially during times of trauma, uncertainty, and when I've felt disconnected from those around me. There have been many moments in my life when I've felt unseen, unheard, or misunderstood. Through self-reflection and writing about my experiences, I've found strength to quiet those self-sabotaging thoughts and move forward as my most authentic self. I genuinely hope my words reflect the power of emotional intelligence as a tool for seeking understanding, healing insecurities, and shedding light on the experiences that shape us, helping each of us become the best version of ourselves and thrive in all our relationships.

Please feel free to keep in touch with me as you continue to Shut Out the Noise and Connect Already. Email me at: authorkristitempleton@gmail.com

Kristi Templeton

Discussion Questions

These questions are meant to provoke introspection and inspire deep conversations about the profound link between self-connection and our relationships with others. Use them for personal reflection in a journal or for thoughtful discussion in a book club setting.

Reflecting on Internal Connection:

1. How do you define "internal connection," and why do you think it's essential for connecting with others?
2. What personal practices or habits can you adopt to deepen your internal connection?
3. How do your emotions, thoughts, and self-awareness influence the way you interact with others?
4. What barriers do you face when trying to connect with yourself, and how might these affect your relationships with others?

Connection with Others:

1. In what ways does deepening your internal connection change how you approach relationships with others?
2. Can you recall a time when you felt truly understood by someone? How did your internal sense of self play a role in that connection?
3. How do you handle conflict in relationships, and how might a stronger internal connection influence the way you approach those situations?

Vulnerability and Authenticity:

1. What does vulnerability mean to you, and how does it tie into both internal connection and building meaningful relationships?
2. How comfortable are you with showing your true self to others, and what do you think holds you back from being more authentic?
3. What impact do you think emotional honesty has on deepening trust in your relationships?

Self-Awareness and Growth:

1. What are some habits or thoughts you notice in yourself that may block genuine connections with others?

2. How does your relationship with yourself (self-acceptance, self-compassion, self-awareness) affect your ability to listen and empathize with others?
3. What role do past experiences and traumas play in shaping how you connect with others today? How can internal work help you address these influences?

The Role of Empathy:

1. How does empathy for yourself translate into empathy for others?
2. What does it mean to "listen" not only to others but also to your own inner voice?
3. Can you think of a time when practicing self-empathy helped you better understand or relate to someone else's struggles?

Exploring Change:

1. What shifts in behavior or mindset have you noticed since beginning to focus on internal connection?
2. How do you think the practice of nurturing internal connection can impact society as a whole?
3. What steps can you take to foster deeper connections within your community based on the principles of internal connection you've learned?

www.ingramcontent.com/pod-product-compliance
Lightning Source LLC
Chambersburg PA
CBHW032111040426
42337CB00040B/188